SANCHIN
Three Battles

Anatomy and Physiology of Sanchin Kata

Pervez B Mistry

(Copyright registration India No.L-58204/2014)

ISBN: 1500961000
ISBN 13: 9781500961008

Dedication

This book is dedicated to my late mom HILLA BEHRAM MISTRY and dad BEHRAM PHIROZSHAW MISTRY who pushed, encouraged and made me what I am today.

To my wife Zeenat without whose constant admonition and encouragement this book would never have been completed.

Accknowledgements

My teachers and especially Shihan Morio Higaonna, whose dedication to Traditional Okinawan Karate-do knows no bounds, and who encouraged me in my research on Sanchin Kata.

To Sensei T. Nakamura for reading my first complete draft.

To Hutoshi Kotwal for her editing and to Khalid Dalvi and Arvind Pandeya for their expertise and help in computer savvy and formatting this book. To Capt. Rustom Vajifdar for the high definition photographs.

To Dr's. Sujeet Rajan and Nauroze Lalkaka, for their going through the entire manuscript and their very complimentary forewords.

To Mr. Gain Hills and his team at Create Space Publishing Company.

To Suverna Jadhav for her drawings and to Cap. Kersi Khambatta for his assistance in partnering me in the photos in this book and last but by no means least, to all my students who have stuck by me these many years.

Sponsor

This book has been sponsored by my very dear friend of many years,

Navzar Jamshed Manekshaw.

Foreword

Congratulations to Sensei Mistry Pervez for publishing the Sanchin Kata book. Sensei Mistry is one of my oldest foreign students who came to Japan back in the 1970s to train at my dojo in the Yoyogi district of Tokyo. He is one of the founding members of our organization (International Okinawan Goju-Ryu Karate-Do Federation, established in 1979) and the first person who brought traditional karate to India. In Indian martial arts society, he is considered as the Father of Karate in India.

He has also practiced several different Japanese Martial Arts such as Judo and Aikido, as well he has a vast knowledge of other martial arts, asian cultures, medicine, modern sports training and sports science.

Sanchin Kata is the most important kata in our style. In olden times, new students would train 3-5 years focusing only on Sanchin before they would learn another kata. It has also been said that this is the oldest kata. This kata was created through the research and experiences of many generations of superb masters. Sanchin kata offers so many benefits to its practitioners, both physically and mentally.

I hope this book encourages its readers to train Sanchin Kata properly and that many people will benefit from this great ancient wisdom.

Morio Higaonna
Seiko Shihan (Supreme Master)
International Okinawan Goju-Ryu Karate-Do Federation

Foreword

I would like to congratulate Sensei Mistry for publishing this very unique book about Sanchin Kata. For Goju Ryu Karate practitioners, Sanchin Kata is the fundamental and essential kata. For many traditional Southern Chinese martial arts, as well as Goju-Ryu and Uechi-Ryu (both of which originated in Fuzhou, China) Sanchin Kata was the most important kata of their style.

After many years of his own training as well as teaching and research in various different cultures and arts, Sensei Mistry reveals many benefits of Sanchin kata, and answers questions regarding why Sanchin is so important. His approach is very scientific and detailed. I believe this book will not only benefit all Goju-Ryu practitioners, but also it would be beneficial for anybody who is interested in health and physical exercise.

Tetsuji Nakamura
World Chief Instructor
International Okinawan Goju-Ryu Karate-Do Federation

Foreword

Pervez Mistry is much more than a Master. Read this book and you will understand why I say this.

If the origins of martial arts began in India with Kallaripayttu from my home state of Kerala (and first documented in the 11th or 12th century AD), then Pervez has taken martial arts to another level with his command and teaching of Sanchin Kata.

Sanchin means 'three battles' and kata is a japanese word describing detailed choreographed patterns of movements practised either solo or in pairs. In Sanchin kata (when properly executed), all the muscles are to be flexed and tensed throughout the kata. This makes it a 'hard' style of karate, and also makes it one of the most strenuous forms of martial arts. In the west, this style of training has only recently been understood and is called as isometric training in bodybuilding.

As a pulmonologist, I always believed I knew everything (everything there was to know at least) about the all-important muscle of breathing, the diaphragm. After meeting Pervez, I realised how little I knew, and how much there was, and still is, to learn. Be it the diaphragm, or the intercostals or any of the accessory muscles of breathing, Pervez's knowledge is more than that of the average pulmonologist. He has mastered the art of understanding as well as teaching breathing techniques – both relaxed and forced - such that they can be practically implemented in day-to-day life to improve one's health and peace of mind.

I have rarely seen art and science so closely linked with the result that this martial art can be so successfully used to better the way we go about our daily lives. On weekday evenings, in the lobby of an old school, his students gather with a certain sense of fervour. There is a palpable sense of passion in all of them as they make and learn new carefully coordinated (and almost perfectly choreographed) moves, and from a sense of fatigue while a city begins to shut down for the day, a renewed energy seems to originate from this group – Sanchin. And when Pervez arrives, there is a fascinating hush and silence – the disciplined respect for the Sensei or Master – the man who teaches based on wisdom from age and experience.

As a doctor specialising in pulmonary medicine, I would encourage many students make Sanchin kata as a part of their daily routine. I am convinced it will help many to cope far better with life's illnesses and stresses.

It will also teach physicians to help patients cope with life's illnesses and stresses much better. And teach physicians to help patient's improve what modern medicine can treat, and bear what modern medicine cannot cure.

Sujeet K. Rajan MD, DNB
Consultant Respiratory Physician

Foreword

I was extremely privileged to be asked by Sensei Pervez Mistry to go through his book on the Sanchin Kata that has been his brain child and passion for several years.

I was requested to ascertain the medical physiological and anatomical facts, and make any corrections and modifications if any. To my surprise I found this treatise to be absolutely faultless. Sensei Pervez Mistry's knowledge of human anatomy and physiology is probably superior to most medical personnel (definitely most of us practicing doctors).

I was also privy to a demonstration of the Sanchin Kata as performed by him. As I watched in awe and admiration, I could see how the breathing regulation and the mental focus on the respiration were actually responsible for accentuating the muscular skeletal performance of all the additional muscles of respiration. It was an exercise in perfection, one of the few experiences that I'm very unlikely to forget in my life.

The Pulmonary Function Tests [PFTs] of so many patients of asthma and other lung diseases also verify that this Kata goes a long way in improving the Vital Capacity and the respiratory reserves of the human system. Even the heart rates and blood pressures of all the practitioners of this art form are lower and better, shockingly even soon after the execution of this kata, emphasizing the relaxing effects of the kata on the entire cardio-respiratory system.

My compliments to Sensei Pervez Mistry for a superbly compiled book.

Dr. Nauroze Lalkaka
MBBS Md.

Content

Introduction

This book has been a long time in becoming a published manuscript. The original 17 page document was written to enable me to deliver a seminar on this kata held in 2007, which was attended by 80 karate-kas from many styles. During the intervening years and many more trips to Okinawa I realized that a serious study on Sanchin was a necessity. There are a few books on Sanchin kata specifically, but none to my knowledge with a scientific understanding on the breathing techniques or on the neuro-muscular combination that this fundamental kata of Goju Ryu employs.

At the outset, I would like to make it very clear that my findings are my responsibility alone and do not in any way reflect those of the institution to which I belong, namely the IOGKF. However I take this opportunity to thank all my mentors from Sensei Barodawalla, my first Ju-jitsu teacher to Kancho Masafumi Suzuki, who not only started my career in Karate-do but also sponsored my very first trip to Kyoto Japan for training at his Seibukan Academy, and finally to my current teacher Shihan Morio Higaonna Seiko Shihan (Supreme Master) IOGKF and all those in between who have shown me the "DO" in Karate.

Let me also state in no uncertain terms, that Sanchin, just as all other Katas, must be practised repeatedly again and again in order to really understand them. A good analogy would be that by reading a book or even a whole library on swimming, you cannot learn to swim unless you get into the water and swim. Whilst this book may help you understand the science of this kata, without its actual practice, this and any other book is useless.

The beauty of this form lies in its simplicity, while the science and its complexity lies in its breathing techniques and neuro-muscular coordination.

Though the original creators of these Goju-Ryu kata are not known, nearly all of these katas were handed down by Hanshi Kanryo Higaonna who had studied and trained under Sensei Ryu Ryuko in Fukien province of China.

It is interesting to note that even in the 21st. Century, most present day styles of Karate-do have a variation of Sanchin kata in their system. For example, Shotokan has Hangetsu; Shito Ryu has Sanchin with the 180° turns, and Uechi Ryu has also sanchin but performed with open hands. All these and other styles emphasize Sanchin training as a must for the attainment of power, speed and clarity of mind and spirit.

In Goju systems today we have essentially two Sanchin katas, the original being handed down by Kanryo Higaonna and the second by Sensei Chogun Miyagi. It is important to note that even Kanryo Higaonna's Sanchin is a variation from the original which was performed with open hands. While preserving the fundamentals of Kanryo Sensei's Sanchin, Miyagi Sensei developed it mainly to complement the original form. It is therefore my understanding that to truly understand and comprehend Sanchin kata, It is of utmost importance to regularly practise both forms of sanchin. However, in this book, I have chosen to explain Sensei Chogun Miyagi's Sanchin kata, as this is the traditional kata of our system.

From the practical point of view, our natural movement is mostly forward, and hardly ever backward, and have therefore developed our muscles and reactions accordingly. Hence, we must practice moving backward, to keep our awareness all around us. Today, in its present form, both types of **Sanchin kata** are taught with the concept of health and fitness, as its **primary** concern.

However as traditionalists, we must also keep in mind and practise the many combat applications of these kata.

From the point of optimum fitness, Karate-do, utilizes all the components of physical training to enable and keep the individual in top physical shape. As Karate instructors, it is helpful to think about physical fitness in relation to the "**specificity of training**", which is that component of training that states that training(sports or traditional) should be both similar and relevant in order to produce better results. It also implies that to improve your current level at a sport or skill, you must perform that sport or skill as well as doing the specific exercises as similar as possible to the sport or skill that will enhance and improve your performance. For example a sprinter would build his thighs and legs for explosive power, or squatting with heavy weights to failure and include plyometric training is his training regime, while a marathon runner would train in muscular endurance like doing a hundred squats. Closer to home, if you want to improve your Sanchin kata, do it as often as you can, and to understand and enhance your technique include chi shi and kongoken training.

Overall fitness may be divided into four categories. They are, "**cardiovascular endurance**", or "**aerobic**" fitness**, "muscular endurance", "muscular power"** and "**flexibility**". Basic actions, and movement drills come under aerobic activity, which is the training for the cardio respiratory fitness, while "**hojo undo**" or Supplementary exercises which use "**chi-shi**" and "**kongo-ken**" (traditional weight training implements) come under "**muscular endurance**" which is the maximum amount of repetitions a muscle or group of muscles can do with a set weight. **Sanchin training** enhances "**muscular endurance**," by improving the capacity to hold a contraction for a length of time without fatigue. "**Muscular power**" is one of the reasons for training in Sanchin kata. **Muscular power** is the ability to lift the heaviest weight you can once. In sanchin training the entire body's muscles are held in an isometric contraction, whilst the limbs perform isotonic movement, which is exactly what happens in a maximum lift, alongwith coordinated breathing that enhances total body power. **"nobi undo" or stretching exercises** completes the fourth and final component of all physical activity. In reference to karate, "muscular endurance" is akin to striking a heavy bag as fast as one can with correct form, while "muscular power" could be explained by striking a makiwara just once with all the power the karateka has.

The beauty and the effectiveness of Goju-Ryu kata, was brought home to me in 1980 during to my first visit to Okinawa. There I witnessed the late Kina Sensei along with the late Sensei An' Ichi Miyagi and Aragaki Sensei, all in their late 60's putting down Go-Dans and Roku-Dans half their age with the greatest of ease during 'Kakaie' training. They later mentioned that they owed their prowess to understanding the Go and Ju aspects of Goju –Ryu, and their daily training in Sanchin and Tensho.

It has always been a source of amazement for me as how the pioneers of karate-do knew, without any of the aids of modern science, that their techniques were scientifically correct. Today with our machines that record heartbeats, brain waves, and other parameters that can record the exact strength of a muscle or group of muscles, or enable us find out the reaction time, speed and impact force, we know beyond a shadow of a doubt that these techniques, handed down through the centuries are not only correct but necessary training tools that may lead us on to levels beyond the physical.

My foremost purpose in writing this book is to give the reader an in-depth understanding of this kata through the physiology of breathing during Sanchin training and the anatomy of the neuro-muscular combination of **"isotonic** and **isometric contractions"** of the muscular system. Hence readers may find it very technical in nature, but without, at the very least, a basic understanding of anatomy and physiology involved, we only touch the surface in our comprehension of Sanchin kata. This book can be used as a reference manual and as a teaching tool enabling one to progress by fully understanding what Sanchin kata is and how it enables one to know and reap the many beneficial effects of Sanchin training.

"He is a good Carpenter who knows his tools".

Chapter I

Understanding Sanchin Kata

1. Introduction

Breath control is critical to the proper performance of breathing katas in Goju Ryu. In karate-do training, both the <u>soft</u> and <u>quiet</u> (nogare and neichai) and the hard and loud (ibuki and waichai) methods of breathing should be employed. In soft breathing, normally practised in the seated position at the beginning and end of a dojo session (mukso), exhale quietly with the tip of the tongue between the teeth and the mouth partially open, while gently forcing the air out through the nose (in yoga manner). During Sanchin and Tensho training, loud breathing is the key as the inhalation is done with the nostrils as if pinched. On exhalation the mouth must be open, with the tip of the tongue placed against the gums of the lower jaw, while forcing out the air as audibly as possible. Note that the audible sound must be the result of expulsion of the breath from the lungs through the compression of the abdominal muscles, and not from the vocal cords of the throat.

2. Mudras in Martial Arts

"Mudras" in Martial Arts of Kung Fu and Karate-do are hand, arm, and body positions meant to stimulate different areas of the body in conjunction with breathing and to affect the flow of vital force in the body. These mudras originated in Hinduism and Buddhism and are identical to the hand, arm and body positions used in karate kata today. In fact Sanchin kata has many of these esoteric "Mudra" hand, and arm positions.

The hidden and symbolic movement of Sanchin occurs when the fists are first crossed by the arms (sankai-gasho) and represents "principles of universal knowledge in a psychological form". In India this symbolization is called *"Mudra "*, in China it is called *"Hsing"*, while in Japan the term given to the hidden symbol is *"In"*. It will be quickly observed too, that nearly all of the movements in Sanchin are mudra. The circular movements of the complete kata relate to and indicate the theory of rebirth or return to the source.

In the form of sanchin, the hands become tools of the Individual will and the arms crossing reflect and are subject to a harmonious or universal will. The internal expansion of the body while inhaling, during performance indicate a desire to rise above earthly ideals, while stabilizing the body during exhalation, reflects the realities of life.

As the fists strike forward powerfully, they create the illusion of an irresistible force pushing out and extinction of all that is evil.

In the original kata handed down by Hanshi Kanryo Higaonna, it is widely accepted that he had changed its original form from the open hand to the presently used closed fists method. Hanshi Kanryo Higaonna returned to Okinawa after 14 years of study with Ryu Ryuko Sensei in 1881. For the first few years, there is no record of his teaching his art to anyone. At the end of this period, and through the influence and support of his friends, Hanshi Kanryo started teaching his art at his home in Naha. He then referred to his art as "Naha-te". At this juncture, he taught Naha-te as a martial art, the ultimate aim of which was to incapacitate the opponent. In September of 1905, at the earnest request of the Principal (Kancho) Junichi Kabayama of the Commercial High School, Sensei Kanryo Higaonna commenced teaching Naha-te as a form of physical, intellectual and moral education. It is probably at this time that he changed the open hand technique of Sanchin Kata to that of the closed fist, as the emphasis had now changed from self-defense to health and fitness, which is still practiced today.

In Kanryo Higaonna's Sanchin Kata, the turning around movement where the head turns first, followed by the body is reminiscent of the owl's ability to turn its head in a half circle; and the owl is suggested, too, by the open eyes and a dead pan expression that should be used during the complete form. It is important to note that Hanshi Chogun Miyagi, the founder of Goju Ryu, had also changed the Sanchin kata, by eliminating the turning movement completely, and completing the form by stepping back. This was done to increase awareness and the sixth sense, to sense an opponent attacking from behind.

To emphasize this special instinctive awareness, I recount two episodes of my early training days. At the Seibukan Academy where I first learned Karate-do, my Sempai Aze San showed me his father's original tanto or fighting knife, and swore me to secrecy as it was forbidden to bring any weapon into the Academy. A half hour later we were joined by our Principal and founder of the Academy, Kancho Masafumi Suzuki. Hardly had a minute passed when he suddenly became aware and said that one of us had a weapon in this room. To this day I have no idea how he knew, and can only attribute it to his training in Karate and specifically in Sanchin and Tensho. Sensei Suzuki also used to perform Sanchin - Tensho as one kata. Whenever he performed these katas either separately or as one, you could literally feel his tremendous power and more so when you saw two deep red circles in the center of his palms.

The second episode took place after a long and arduous session in Tokyo, when we were all returning to our respective homes or hotels, traveling by train. Shihan Morio Higaonna was fast asleep when the train stopped at his station, he still had not awakened. Suddenly one of the students realized this and he shouted out at Shihan that this was his station. At this point the automatic doors of the compartment were starting to close, and in one smooth coordinated movement Shihan's one hand grasped his bag above him on the rack and the other hand onto another bag between his legs, and in one "tsuri ashi" movement (side sliding) in neko ashi dachi (cat stance) he was out onto the platform waving back to us as the train moved on. On sudden awakening from deep sleep, there is always a few seconds of disorientation. Here there was none, only instant awareness translated into instant action.

Shihan Morio Higaonna, my sensei for the past 35 years, and one of the most respected karatekas in the world, further explains that in normal life, we naturally move forward and as such have developed our muscles and instincts accordingly. Hence when moving backward we must concentrate on what we are doing as it is not a movement we do naturally. It was to develop this type of backward awareness and movement, that Chogun Miyagi Sensei possibly revised Kanryo Higaonna Sensei's original Sanchin kata. As Shihan Higaonna has often explained that it is a natural tendency to shorten our steps when we move backward as opposed to when we move forward. In the Sanchin kata of Chogun Miyagi Sensei, it is of great importance to keep the same length of step while moving backward as we use for the forward movements. It is for this reason that at the end of the kata, we must return to our original position.

We presently use the closed fist in the practice of Sanchin. Prior to introduction of the closed fist in Sanchin kata in Okinawa by Kanryo Higashinonna (fist saint), the entire kata was always performed with open hands.

A major reason for the enhancement of our system of karate is our Katas of **"breathing and meditation in action."** Meditation has always been associated with sitting in one place(stillness) and focusing on breath or your navel or assuming a state of "no mind" (as in Zen meditation).

I have been doing this Kata well over 21 years and for the last 10 years nearly every morning. In spite of the tremendous contraction of all the body muscles and movement, at the completion of this kata, I am completely relaxed with a mental state that I can only describe as peaceful, and with an overall sense of heightened awareness.

The vital fuel for life is breath, and logic tells us that when mental or physical exertion occurs, breathing becomes difficult and more blood (and thus more oxygen) is retaken from the inhaled air, and one can rapidly become extremely exhausted. To keep exhaustion to the minimum and to best utilize the oxygen brought into the system, the breathing method in Sanchin kata should be utilized:

Inhale through the nose, taking a deep breath into the lower stomach. This is easier said than done. Most people lock the breath in the chest rather than pushing it deeper into the lower chest whilst imagining that the air is pushed into the lower abdomen. At this moment the entire body should be taut and under noticeable muscular tension.

Then, slowly start exhaling by forcing all of the air out of the body through the mouth, squeezing with stomach muscles allowing the diaphragm to move upward to its normal position. Only when all of the air is expelled should inhaling commence again. When this is done breathing out through the mouth, it is called "ibuki" (Naha method).

Observe the following points:

1. All hand movements must be accomplished with tension whilst breathing in and out.
2. There must be no relaxing and lifting movements of the shoulders and, or the pelvis once the kata is commenced.
3. Middle block positions require the elbows to be inside of the rib cage, with the elbows about the width of one fist from the body and hands must be just within the alignment of the upper arms.
4. Exhale as you strike or block, keeping a constant tension in the entire body, for the entire duration of the kata performance.
5. When performing the form, clear the mind of all distractions.
6. Breathing and action must be totally coordinated, commencing and ending simultaneously.

The breathing techniques are examined in detail in Chapter I-8, under 'Physiology of Respiration".

3. History: Sanchin Kata Through The Ages

"Erh-Iu-chuan" was the ancient Chinese name given to this kata, which has experienced only moderate changes in performance since its inception nearly thirteen centuries ago by Zen Buddhist monks. Sanchin has also been known through its historical years by the name *"Chi schich"* and *"San schich"*. In Okinawa, the name refers to the eighteen techniques of hand movement used to train students while using also the abdominal breathing and the theories of intrinsic energy to defeat their opponents. In an esoteric sense the term refers to the bond between emotions and passions. Sanchin kata is also referred to as the kata of the "Three Battles of Life" or the constant strife between the soul, mind, and body or even the three conflicts, birth, survival, and death. From a more practical point of view Sanchin may also

refer to the three main target areas; namely: *jodan*; *chudan* and *gedan* (Face; Body; and Groin).

Zen buddhist monks at China's ancient Shaolin monastery and temple, developed martial arts and meditation beginning nearly 1,700 years ago. One of these Monks was "Bhodidharma" who left India in or around 537 A.D. He was the third son of a south Indian king, and hence well versed in

Kalarypyatt

the martial arts of south India namely **"KALARYPYATT"**. He had in all probability also learned the art of **"ASTHANGA YOGA"** or yoga for warriors, which is unlike the static positions used in other forms of Hatta Yoga, and utilizes special breathing techniques during its performance. It is therefore quite probable that seeing the lack of physical fitness of the monks at the Shaolin monastery, he used these the techniques of Kalaripyat and Asthanga yoga along with seated meditation techniques that were already in use. In seeking satori (complete oneness with self and nature); they recognized and accepted the two paths open to that goal; one through the practise of sitting Zen and the other through the practice of moving Zen. Sitting Zen is based on stillness (meditation), while moving or standing Zen depends upon action. Both practices are a single internal reality being practiced and viewed from two different view points. Standing Zen helps to discipline the practitioner's control while at the same time developing physical and mental energies. Over many years, the standing Zen method, focusing energy toward reaching a stage of enlightenment through physical superiority, evolved into the way of martial arts practice known as Sanchin (Erh-Iu-chuan). "The roots of **"Saamchin"** (as it is called in China) date back to the Taoists of ancient China. Abhorring the nature of their society they became mountain recluses and tried to live in harmony with nature.

Saamchin was developed to build, contain and release one's power **(KI)**, thus emphasizing and regulating the flow of air and synchronizing it with the expansion (floating) and contraction (sinking) of muscular activity.

Master Wu Bin, of China's Wushu Research Institute, considers exercises like the Saamchin vitally important in mobilizing the inner circulation of air flow to reach out to the extremities in order to bring together one's external and internal forces.

In short, Saamchin teaches one about the summation of total joint forces: how to bring everything together, while at the same time, unleashing great amounts of power. It is also a way in which to keep the body electrically charged and physically in tune. Done correctly using diaphragm and abdominal breathing techniques similar to certain techniques in "Pranna" or breathing techniques of Yoga. It should not cause undue strain rather it should massage one's inner organs and invigorate the body.

Saamchin did not take on a combative element until it was adopted by Shaolin recluses much later in history.

The Kanji of Sanchin

Whilst Saamchin self-defense applications vary from school to school, the exercise employs the techniques of deflecting, and attacking with piercing blows to various vital points, seizing and most importantly, throwing and trapping.

It is my personal opinion that the roots of Sanchin Kata may have evolved from the **"Pranayama"** or breathing techniques of Hatta Yoga. There are more than 50 pranayama techniques, and they fall under specific categories. To cure specific ailments and even disease; to abolish ignorance and to attain concentration and meditation; and also to prolong life; and to acquire phenomenal strength and imperviousness to pain. With reference to this last category, and due to the exchange of knowledgebetween China and India, it is likely that some pranayama techniques form the roots of present day Sanchin.

At this point, I must stress that any form of breathing done incorrectly could have serious consequences, and Sanchin Kata is no exception. Hence for beginners, the concentration should be focused only on the stance and hand actions and not on the breath. Breathing for beginners must be kept soft and not under pressure. Though sanchin is performed in a group class, the Instructor must take each individual separately and alone since each individual is different, especially during "SHIME" or testing during the performance of this kata. If an Individual is strong and has been practising sanchin for a long time then the instructor may increase the force of his blows and resistance. If the practitioner is a beginner, then only resistance should be applied without the slapping blows. This also holds good for women and youngsters.

There are several references where Hanshi Chogun Miyagi has called Sanchin an "external" or hard form and also referred to "Tensho" as internal or the soft, form. Similarly, these pranayama techniques have been classified in the YOGA SUTRAS as: External (Bhaya), Internal (Abhyantra) and Retention (Kumbhaka), which incidentally, are to be determined according to internal organs (Desh), Time (Kala), and number (Sankhya). These may probably be the roots of Chinese Medicine and Meridian Theory.

4. The Neuro Musculosketal System

Introduction

Although knowledge of the major anatomical systems is important for all those involved in serious physical activity, and more so in teaching the same, the system most directly affected by any movement is the muscular system, for it is the contraction and relaxation of specific muscles that enables us to block, punch kick, and in general to engage in combat.

We are the product of over two million years of evolutionary history, and in all this time, the essence of muscular management has been that a certain amount of load or force acts against a group of muscles, some of the muscles, or all muscles of the human body. There are three types of muscles tissue: skeletal, cardiac and visceral.

Skeletal muscles are voluntary muscles, which means that they can be made to contract by conscious effort.

Cardiac muscles form the walls of the heart and are involuntary by nature.

Visceral muscles are found in the walls of the internal organs like the stomach and the intestine and the blood vessels. The contraction of the visceral muscles is also involuntary.

Sanchin breathing invigorates the internal organs due to diaphragmatic and abdominal pressure and the high levels of oxygen flowing in and the carbon dioxide flushing out. This keeps all the internal organs within the thoracic and pelvic cavities healthy and highly functional.

In our art of Karate-Do we essentially deal with the human body, mind and spirit. Unfortunately, most of us merely act as drivers and chauffeurs rather than knowledgeable mechanics. For those of us at the Instructors level, it is vital to have a basic knowledge of the human body. It is not my intent to make you an expert in anatomy, physiology and kinesiology, but to give you a greater understanding of just how the body works and specifically what happens to it during sanchin training.

It is very obvious that any action we do from twitching our right little pinky to the most complex movement in a kata is the result of our musculoskeletal system. It allows us to breathe, move, twist and bend, to do summersaults, flips and to achieve strength, control, and grace in the performance of the kata. However, this is only the tip of the iceberg. Our bones and muscles are articulated and in total control by the nervous system. In combination, these two systems are known as the Neuro-Musculosketal system. It also protects and contains our internal organs.

This system is the body's control center and network for all internal communication by stimulating and controlling movement. For example, when you decide to lie down on the mat from a standing position, consciously or automatically this is what takes place in a mater of seconds. The decision to lie down takes place in your brain. Then the nervous system (NS) sends the message to your thighs and leg muscles to relax and bend at the knee joints. A few mili-seconds later gravity takes over till your bottom touches the mat while at the same time the NS commands other muscles to counter act gravity and keep you from falling like a sack of potatoes. As soon as your bottom touches the mat, the NS allows these and other muscles to relax enabling you to un-fold and lie down on to the mat. Muscle tissue continuously gives the skeletal system this support even at rest. For example in a seated position, the body is also using muscle activity to hold the head upright, to balance on the buttocks, and to keep limbs in a position of rest. This takes place because of the contraction and relaxation of the muscles through the command and reception of your brain and nervous system.

Skeletal Muscle

A muscle is made of many thousands of fibers, each thinner than a hair on your head and consists of the fleshy part or belly of a muscle encased by connective tissue fibers that end into tendons usually at both ends. All skeletal muscles are voluntary muscles, and can be made to contract (shorten or tensed) by conscious effort. And this is exactly what happens during sanchin training.

In his book, "The History of Okinawan Karate" the Author, Sensei Morio Higaonna recounts the time when Sensei Kanryo

Higaonna was called upon to demonstrate his Sanchin kata versus that of another Sensei by the name of Kojo in what is referred to as a Sanchin "Saiban" or Court. This was presided over by a doctor from the Okinawan Prefectural Hospital. Both the Sensei's performed the Sanchin Kata one after another, with the doctor probing and prodding and observing each detail with great care. The following is taken from Sensei's Book:

"For example, when Kojo performed Sanchin, his abdominal area was tensed in a vertical direction like a paper lantern, whereas Higaonna's abdomen was tensed by rolling the abdomen up and in a spiraling motion, concentrating all the power in his tanden. His testicles were then retracted up into the groin area where they were protected". The Doctor then announced his decision that the Sanchin of Kanryo Higaonna was superior.

Fig. 1.	Fig. 2.	Fig. 3.	Fig. 4.
Relaxed abdominal.	Tensed abdominal..	Tensed abdominal with relaxed solar plexus	Tensed & rolled up abdominal with solar plexus contracted.

The abdominal muscle group consists of the Rectus Abdominus, the external and internal oblique muscles and most importantly the transverse abdominus muscles, all collectively known today as the 'core'. By contracting the abdominal area most people with good physique can show off their six packs or even take a hard punch in this region. However, if you punch or even just poke them in the lower abdomen just above the pubic bone they will go down hard. What Sensei Kanryo Higaonna had done was to contract the entire abdominal muscle group including the transverse abdominus or the entire CORE of the body or the human corset. This type of muscular control where the entire abdomen from the solar plexus to the pubis and even the kidneys are protected, is far harder to attain than merely contracting the abdominal or six-pack area, and can be achieved through regular Sanchin Kata practice, as will be explained in the chapters concerning performance.

Muscle tissue has the ability to receive and respond to any input from the nervous system, which would cause the muscle to contract (shorten or thicken) or relax (lengthen). It also has the ability to be stretched as muscles have elasticity. From the view point of training, it is important to understand that most muscles of the trunk and extremities are arranged in opposing pairs. This is when one muscle is contracting to achieve the desired movement **the agonist,** its opposite muscle the **antagonist** is being stretched. For example during a **mai-geri** (front kick) the quadriceps muscle (the agonist) is contracted whilst the ham-string muscle (the antagonist) is being stretched. At most joints, several muscles help by combining their support to perform the same movement and are known as **synergists and other muscles which aid in holding the desired position are called fixators.**

Isotonic and isometric movement

These are terms normally used in exercise terminology though they may also be used in normal activity. The term **isotonic** means the shortening of a muscle under a constant load which relates to movement of the limb or part of the body performing the action. In short, when a limb is bent while performing a exercise or a movement it is called "isotonic". Some examples are the bicep curl, the tricep extension; ham string curls and leg extensions. In Karate-do all the actions of blocking, punching and kicking come under this heading. An **isometric** exercise refers to holding still under substantial or maximum load, or in other words a movement or exercise where the limb concerned is not bent. Some Yoga postures are examples of this category. In Sanchin kata whilst the arms perform **isotonic** movement, the body is held in an **isometric** position throughout the performance.

It is interesting to note that when the human embryo begins to develop, it is the **heart and central nervous system** which include the brain and spinal cord that receive the primary attention. Everything else comes later and this becomes obvious when one realizes that it is through the brain and nervous system that we are able to perceive and evaluate our environment and at the same time are able to control the body as well as direct its activities and successfully survive.

5. The Nervous System

The Nervous System is essential to sensory-perception, feeling pain and pleasure, control of movement and the regulation of all body functions such as breathing, digestion, assimilation and other autonomous functions.

This is the body's most important and complex network. It is also vital for the development of thought, memory and language. It comprises the brain and the spinal cord which ultimately control all the nervous tissue of the other parts of the body.

In the course of sanchin training, our nervous system is in constant two way communication between the brain and via the spinal cord to every other part of the body. To allow this (NS) to work, do not count the number of steps or the number of hand action in order to do the form correctly. This is incorrect, as it inhibits the development of perception, awareness, and the sixth sense. In short, one must do the kata through the essence of feeling, rather thak thinking, where conscious thought is absent, and the mind is focused on one's breathing.

This leads us to the **autonomic nervous system** (**ANS**) which is responsible for the maintenance and control of the involuntary actions in the body. For example, the **heart,** a smooth muscle, is regulated by the part of the nervous system that does not require conscious thought, but still receives directions from the brain, and it does not think about the heart beat, it happens because there is a specific part of the brain known as the autonomic nervous system. Every part of the body, whether controlled by conscious thought or hormonal release, is technically controlled by the brain. Here adjustments are made automatically by the brain's response to stimuli. During exercise or any sport, the **ANS** sends a signal to the heart to beat faster with greater force so that the body can cope during this level of activity.

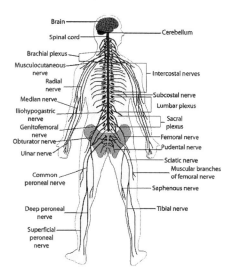

Whenever part of the body functions or moves as the direct result of the thought, it does so as a result of **EFFERENT IMPULSES**, or nerve impulses that start in the brain to any and all tissues and organs in all parts of the body via the spinal cord.

When we become aware of something in our environment, without using our sight (such as your fingers on a key board) we do so because of the **AFFERENT IMPULSES** that brought you that information from the tips of your fingers to your brain via the spinal cord. Of importance to all those involved in any form of physical activity is the nervous system's function of stimulating and controlling movement. Skeletal muscle cannot contract unless it is stimulated by a nerve impulse. Without a command from the brain and/or the spinal cord, coordinated movements such as the performance of a kata are not possible.

The single nervous system that we all have may be divided into two categories as per their location; the **central nervous system (CNS)** which consists of the brain and the spinal cord and the **peripheral nervous system (PNS)** which are long fibre nerves that connect to all parts of the body. These nerves include *'motor neurons'*, and initiate our voluntary movement, especially the control of our muscles as in all our Kata and more so in Sanchin kata. It also contains the '*Sympathetic & Para Sympathetic Nervous System*', which in turn control all our involuntary functions. The **CNS** is the command center of the entire nervous system as it receives all the information from the **peripheral nervous system (PNS)** and assembles this information, and then creates a fitting response. In other words during sanchin and tensho training, once the katas are learned, all actions take place without conscious thought however the breathing action works consciously, unlike other Katas where the actions and breathing take place sub-consciously or autonomously.

6. Reflexes

There are many reasons for training in martial arts, and one of the most important is to be able to defend yourself and others who may not be capable of doing so.

In order to accomplish, this many thousands of repetitions of defense and attack are necessary before they become as fast as a reflex action. If you face an attacker with a knife and start to think whether you should kick him or hit him, scream for help, or turn and run, you may end up seriously injured if not dead. However, if you have trained in knife defense, your eyes will perceive the threat and your body will already be responding with the right attack without any conscious thought, and that is precisely why those many thousands of repetitions are required. Our bodies through evolution already have such a system in place known as *"reflexes"* or unconscious motor response to sensory stimuli, which occur at the spinal level.

"Uchikomi" in Judo parlance is the repetitive practice of moving in and out of a throw 50 or even a hundred, times in every training session which I used to do in my early Judo training days. One day I was walking down Colaba Causeway, a famous shopping area of Bombay as it was know then, I suddenly felt a hard slap on my shoulder, and without any conscious thought, I bent low grabbed the hand lifting and pulling my adversary over my shoulder. As my assailant's body flew over my shoulder I heard a familiar expletive in our Parsee language and instantaneously realized that my *"attacker"* was a elderly close family friend, so I righted up and he landed on his feet instead of on his back. My profound apologies were not enough and to the vast amusement of his friend and pass-ersby's, I got a mouthful of the more colorful side of our Parsee language. The more important point here, is the second I felt the hard slap on my shoulder from behind, I reacted instinctively without conscious thought, the end result of many hours of training.

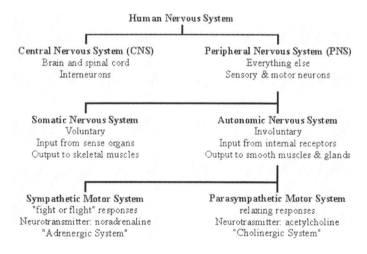

The **reflex arc** is ingeniously designed to help keep the body safe, as it is this unit that permits immediate responses to danger related stimulus. A reflex arc is in fact the simplest and most primitive nerve pathway in the body. It includes a *receptor*, a *sensory neuron*, a *motor neuron* and *an* integrating *center* within the spinal cord, a motor neuron that relays the impulses back out to a muscle, and the muscular response that finishes the action. There is a very short route for the sensory neurons to travel to reach the motor neurons and to maintain the shortest route possible, only two or three neurons are involved in a reflex arc.

The Somatic Reflex

These reflexes are those that include some involvement of the skeletal muscles. These reflexes are divided into three categories, each named after the response they produce. They are: *1. The stretch Reflex; 2. The withdrawal reflex and 3. An intersegmental reflex.*

The Stretch Reflex

This is also sometimes referred to as the **myotatic stretch reflex.** The sense organs or neural receptors responsible for the stretch reflex are the muscle spindles lying parallel to the muscle fiber, and the **golgi tendon organs** (GTO) found deep within the muscle-tendon junctions. Each of these receptors is sensitive to stretch and aids in protecting a muscle against unnecessary injury. Generally speaking, the muscle spindle follows the movements of its adjacent muscle fibers. Hence, as the muscle fiber stretches, so does the spindle. However, if the stretch is extreme, the muscle spindle responds by sending a signal to the spinal cord, which returns an order to create a sudden, protective muscular contraction. The spindle ceases to fire when this contraction begins, as the muscle fiber contracts, thus preventing muscle tissue tear or injury. An example of a myotatic stretch reflex is when the Doctor taps you just below the knee which results in a jerk of the lower leg also called the "knee-jerk reflex". In fact you are aware of it consciously only because separate receptors for the sensation of touch send messages to the cerebral cortex and into your conscious mind. This will be explained in more detail later.

Most sports that involve dynamic shocks use this reflex, even though the sportsmen involved may not be aware of it. In Karate training, when you do a series of jump kicks, the muscle spindles in the knee extensors of the thigh are stretched by the impact of your feet hitting the dojo floor, and absorbing one landing after another would very quickly collapse, if it were not for the myotatic stretch reflex. In fact what happens is that each impact activates the reflex for the quadricep femoris muscle within fractions of a second and thus keeps the body in an upright position.

The Withdrawal Reflex

Also called a *flexor reflex,* and If you have ever touched a hot pan or iron and reflexively jerked away you have inadvertently performed a withdrawal reflex. The pain sensation has set the whole reflex into instant action. The receptor responds and sends the information via sensory neurons. It reaches the spinal cord and sends the information and the associated neurons take over and pass it to the motor neurons within the muscles involved which then contract to produce a withdrawing snapping action. Additionally and simultaneously, the antagonistic muscles relax, otherwise they may inhibit the body's ability to snap the muscles to withdraw. In Sanchin Shime, this is the reflex we consciously learn to block out, when slapped hard on the shoulders, so as to foster a calm mind.

This reflex is naturally enhanced by the practice of one-step sparring repeatedly with a partner. Whilst one person does a face punch taking one step forward in the forward stance, the other partner retreats one step backward with a corresponding face block, then immediately steps forward an attacks with a face punch while his partner steps back with a face block. This should be repeated non-stop for 2 to 3 minutes.

The Intersegmental Reflex

Indulge in a pleasant walk on any of Mumbai's beaches, and if you step on a broken shard of glass, (which is more likely than not) you will have just initiated the *intersegmental reflex*. This action is vital in maintaining balance during a flexor response, and is also called the crossed extensor reflex. So coming back to our walk on the beach, the second you step on the sharp piece of glass, there is ample crossing of information, as the opposite side of your body will take over to maintain balance, while withdrawing your foot. At the same time, your body will inhibit other muscles during such a reflex in order to further maintain your balance.

These are reflexes that are designed specifically for maintaining physiological function (such as urination) and numerous reflexes that are designed to help the body avoid injury, or prevent further injury.

When you first learnt to drive a car, you had to consciously think of putting your foot on the brake to stop the car. After many years of driving a car now, that action would be automatic. Why? Because you have built up the synapses and they have formed shortcuts to your motor neurons which command the flexor muscles of your right leg to hit the brakes, whilst at the same time you may swing the wheel, and change gear, in a further effort to aid in stopping the car and avoiding an accident.

This same process takes place throughout your many years of karate training. The thousands of punches, blocks, and kicks and the many hours of kata practice, will come in useful in the event of a sudden attack, just like a reflex action.

The breathing katas of our system enhance these reflexes. The high oxygen volume charges the body and the isometric tension increases the awareness of all sensory input. Equally important, during "shime" the body learns **NOT** to react and thereby learns to decrease the pain threshold. This also teaches the practitioner to control and decrease his / her pain threshold level.

7. Fight or Flight the Hormonal System

Understanding stress

Many of the body's functions are controlled by the "**endocrine**" glands which help to keep the various parts of the body working in harmony with each other. In his book **"The Tao of Jeet-Kun-do"** Bruce Lee often refers to what he calls **"controlled emotional anger"**. We all know that emotions can play a very major role with our physical abilities. It is the power of this imagination that triggers the hormones which when confronted with a life threatening situation, could turns us into fighting tigers, or on the other hand, make us flee like the proverbial deer. Psychologically speaking, this is termed as the "**fight or flight response**".

By secreting the chemicals known as "**hormones**" into the blood stream, they are able to relay messages to organs to carry out specific processes which include such critical activities as growth and reproduction. Since all hormones are concerned with metabolism, they tend to interact with one another to bring about the desired end.

The stress our Ancestors faced was simple and of short duration – kill or be killed or eat or be eaten - and the end, one way or the other, came quickly. In sudden, life threatening situations we still react much the same way our ancestors did.

However, present day stress lasts much longer, worries for ourselves, our families, our jobs, and a whole lot of other stress builders, day after day, often take a heavy toll in the lives of individuals and even whole families.

One of the most important benefits of regular sanchin training lies in its ability in reducing this long term stress and in maintaining a positive attitude. Adrenaline junkies or people who love to get a high from dangerous sports like sky-diving, base jumping, and car or bike racing, thrive on this type of short duration stress, which is and can often be stimulating. Long term constant exposure to stress can be and often is deadly. The symptoms are constant fatigue, anxiety, eventually leading to severe depression, and possibly death.

After sanchin training, the forced inhalation and exhalation relaxes the blood vessels and allows circulation to the extremities and this in turn gets the oxygen and nutrients to all the organs and body tissues.

Sanchin training regularly helps to deal with the effects of stress by inducing the nervous system to function at peak level bringing awareness and frees the accumulated stress in the body. This stress response is a primitive response to a threatening or dangerous situation and has been of primary importance in ensuring the continued survival of the human species. As mentioned earlier, we are the product of more than two million years of evolution. The survival of the human race has depended on quick physical responses to dangers and it is with the repeated practice of Sanchin training that the trainee may be able to harness these chemical messengers.

However, in our society today, we cannot take the law into our own hands. To attack the driver of the car that has cut you from the wrong side, would invariably result in legal hassles, while fleeing from a tense board meeting would in all probability be perceived as being mentaly unstable.

The body's physiological response to danger

One of the important reasons that the human species has survived so far, is thanks to the body's innate reaction to a life threatening situation. This is governed by the most primitive part of the brain normally referred to as the "lizard brain", or the hypothalamus. This governs our base emotions; anger, jealousy; and what we would consider as "our space". Earlier all stress was believed to be a result of outside pressure on an individual, otherwise why would one person react calmly to a similar situation while another would probably collapse? A person trained in martial arts has the knowledge and the many hours of practice to save himself from a dangerous situation.

Take my case for example; I was returning home from a friend's house on my Yamaha 350 cc bike, on Mumbai's Walkeshwar Road, which is one of the few slopes in our city. As I turned the corner going downhill, I saw a car and two bikes racing each other coming uphill. There was no time to swerve and the car hit my crash-bar and I was flying over the car. I distinctly remember telling myself to tuck and somersault, which resulted in me landing on my feet, and thereafter collapsing in a heap. What I realized only later, was that the crash-bar had jammed my right foot between it and the foot rest pedal, and the impact had fractured most of my metatarsals of my foot. Had I not had the training in Judo to fall, roll, somersault I doubt if I would be writing this book. From a practical point of view, it was the many hours and continued practice of *"Ukemi"* (Falling practice in Judo) that contributed to saving myself, but I also believe that Sanchin training helped in my choosing instantaneously the correct response.

Sanchin is often referred to as "moving meditation". The difference between the other katas and the breathing katas is that in the former the practitioner visualizes an opponent while in the latter there is only focus on the breathing and the mind is alert.

When confronted by a life threatening situation our eyes perceive the danger which initiates two branches of the **central nervous system(CNS)** the sympathetic and the parasympathetic nervous systems. The former commences the process of the hormonal and chemical defense systems by releasing a deluge of hormonal secretions. On recognizing the danger the hypothalamus triggers the pituitary gland which in turn releases hormones that make the adrenal gland flood the body with adrenalin. This massive dose has different reactions in different parts of the body. In the muscles it increases blood flow to allow for instant action; in the stomach and intestines it decreases the blood flow since digestion is not needed in time of danger. It also increases the blood supply to the brain and relaxes the air ways to improve respiration, which speeds up the heart allowing blood circulation to all the extremities, and fuel from glucose, fats, or stored insulin is released to provide additional energy. This stimulates the body and increases blood pressure.

Sanchin training, through its breathing technique and muscular contraction, prepares the body to enhance the innate defense mechanisms in our bodies. It also trains us to remain calm in an emergency.

8. Posture & Movement

Introduction

Posture is one of the most important aspects of health but unfortunately it is also the most neglected aspects in daily life. For sportsmen, martial artists, dancers, and those into any form of exercise it becomes vital to have a good posture. If your posture is inherently poor, your foundation will also be structurally bad, which will diminish your strength and also to a large extent make your natural body movements uncoordinated and eventually lead to a collapse partially or even completely. For people who essentially live sedentary lives, poor posture will sooner than later lead to frozen shoulders, severe pain in the neck and back, bad knees, and a host of other aches and pains. Sanchin training lays the foundations for good posture, and even helps in giving relief from cervical, thoracic, and lumbar pain.

Ninety percent of aches and pains of mature adults are the end results not of injuries or affliction but due to the long term effects of distortion in posture and / or mental depression that may have taken place during childhood or adolescence.

If the child has bad or crooked teeth, braces are put on, usually for cosmetic purposes. But what about our bodies? What we have come to think of as aches or pains of middle and old age are actually a result of bad posture during childhood. The posture or body alignment of the child or teenager which should have been periodically examined and corrected throughout the growing years, was and still is neglected. If corrected early in life, the short term benefits are that the child will look and feel better and be less likely to suffer muscle injuries. He / she will also be able to recoup and rehabilitate much faster. An age old saying, in posture therapy is "*Bones go where muscles put them, bones stay where muscles keep them*"

We are all born with perfect posture and an equally perfect breathing rhythm. Watch a year old child old child and see how they sit, crawl, stand, walk, and squat. The head is in perfect natural position in relation to the spine. Their breathing is in perfect synch to their activity, whether sitting standing squatting or walking.

Unfortunately we loose this natural ability as we grow older, since it happens on a subconscious level as we tend to imitate our parents and elders.

"*Stand up straight; Don't Slouch; Sit up straight*"

These are the normal cursory commands of concerned parents. Unfortunately most parents think that posture is voluntary and just a matter of discipline. Even in the medical community, health care professionals have vague answers to anything that is not a disease or cannot be treated with drugs or surgery.

Good posture or the correct posture is not just a voluntary matter and children, teenagers and adults don't usually outgrow posture problems. Over a period of time the wrong posture then becomes the "natural posture" of the child, teenager and adult. To correct this malady it must be remembered that changing the alignment requires adjusting and / or lengthening of all the soft tissues within the area to be corrected.

Most of the adults whom I've treated for pain had posture problems dating back to their adolescence. Most of them have wished that they could have been corrected when they were still children.

The rules of good posture

- Bones go where muscles put them, bones stay where muscles keep them.
- The body works as one complete unit and the body is only as strong as its weakest component.
- No body part is as strong as the whole body.
- Your ankle pain may actually be due to a habit of leaning the neck forward and drooping shoulders. Treat the body as a whole not in parts.
- The seat of your power lies in your lower abdomen or core or what in Japanese is called "Tanden".
- Do not sacrifice your health for bigger muscles, more strength or greater speed.
- Always choose the middle ground; extremes in either direction are dangerous. Remember to keep the balance.
- Do not be ashamed of your body, rather be proud of your body and look after it.

Postural Alignment & Treatment

The correct standing posture is actually a question of perfect balance between the upper torso, the hips and the legs. It does not mean standing at attention ramrod stiff, but rather a relaxed position with hip slightly tucked forwards no more than 10 degrees in men and fifteen degrees in women. The shoulders should be straight and pulled just a little way back, with the weight on the shoulder blades rather than on the shoulder joints or the trapezius muscles and the inner edge of each shoulder blade should be equidistance from the the spine. The feet should be about shoulder width wide with the knees slightly flexed and not locked. In walking, the legs should swing freely forward without twisting to one side or the other, and the arms should swing freely in inverse coordination with the legs.

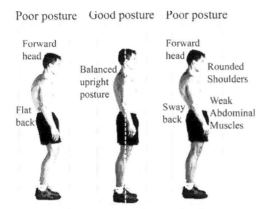

Poor posture   Good posture   Poor posture

Forward head | Balanced upright posture | Forward head | Rounded Shoulders

Flat back | Sway back | Weak Abdominal Muscles

Hunched, Normal and Sway-back posture

This is a description of a body that is balanced and well aligned in relation to gravity. In other words, a body should be able to use gravity, rather than constantly fighting it. A body that is unbalanced will be using a great deal of energy going constantly against gravity, and ultimately gravity will be the final victor. Furthermore, when posture is incorrect, the muscles and tissues which are holding the body out of alignment are in a constant state of suffering that becomes worse with the passage of time. For this reason, therapy done to correct this situation can more easily, comfortably, and effectively be carried out from time to time, beginning in childhood and continuing through adolescence and into adulthood.

For those of us actively engaged in Sports in general and Karate-do in particular, **postural correctness or a symmetrical posture** where the left and right sides of the body are equally strong; where the back of the body is as strong as the front; and the upper body is also as strong as the lower body, is of paramount importance. For example, if a beginner student has a cervical tilt (neck leaning to one side or a forward extension) his/her shoulder will correspondingly will be more raised than the other shoulder, and this in turn will result in one arm being slightly longer than the other by about an inch. When this student performs a forward straight punch(oi-tsugi in zenkutsu dachi), there will be tremendous and unnatural strain on the deficient side of the body, creating a torque or twist in the rotator cuff or the shoulder muscles, which if not remedied, could result in a serious shoulder injury.

Muscles of the Rotator Cuff

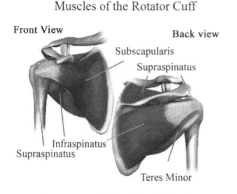

Anatomy of the Shoulder &
Rotator cuff Muscles

In any aspect of karate our shoulders are constantly used and without learned control, any overhead activity, and even the simple act of lifting the arm, would and does result in injury. When the arm is pulled back in preparation for a punch, most beginners tend to lift the shoulder joint, and this is very evident in Sanchin, as the movement is slow and easily noticeable. The muscle group we rely on for this control are the **Rotator Cuff Muscles.**

With repeated training, the beginner learns to place the shoulder blades (scapula) in their neutral position which is about 3 to 4 inches from the top of the trapezius muscle. Now on punching or blocking the bigger and far more powerful muscles of the lats and chest are involved. This results in power and speed without the risk of injury.

The larger and more powerful muscles that generate movement of the arm are the deltoids, latissimus dorsi (one of the most important muscles in all tsugi and uke waza and especially in sanchin training) and the chest muscles. If you are suffering from a chronic shoulder injury, or after surgery or trauma, try this out. The rotator cuff muscles are dependent on the proper positioning of the shoulder blades (scapula) for effective control. If the scapula is angled too far forward or upward (rounded or drooping shoulders) as is normally the case for most weight lifters and body builders, these shoulder and upper arm muscles become over strained and may fail to keep the shoulder joint centered. The role of these muscles therefore is to maintain the position of the shoulder joint while the larger muscles (lats and chest) generate power. Following is the way to rectify drooping shoulders and an end to pain and undue suffering:

Facing a mirror, sit comfortably on a stool with the feet on the floor about hip width apart with hands resting on your thighs. Look straight ahead retaining the natural curve of your neck, rib cage and lumbar spine (small of the back area). Holding this position and breathing naturally, gently retract your shoulder blades towards each other. This action is done by gently pulling your shoulders backwards. Now watch your shoulders in the mirror and they should be in a straight line and not one above or below the other. Hold this position for 10 seconds initially and increase the time until it becomes your natural position. Once you get comfortable in this position, now start positioning your arms, forward, overhead and laterally outward, keeping the shoulder blades in their neutral position. When this action becomes natural your trap muscles will be relaxed and finally pain free.

The Lumbar curve

A great percentage of people also have an excessive **"lordotic"** curve, or the small of the back area. Any excessive curvature in this region, will eventually lead to anything from a mild uncomfortable feeling to severe pain and could be due to several reasons; a genetic anomaly, an ever increasing stomach, an accident, or just plain bad posture.

This puts a great strain on the Lumbar area of the spinal column and eventually leads to a ruptured disk in this region. If a person with this imbalance were to perform a zenkutsu dachi, he/she would automatically arch his/her back even more, and thereby putting greater pressure on the already afflicted area. The end result, I leave to your fertile imagination. However, Okinawan Goju Ryu Karate emphasizes the importance and has laid down the foundations of correct stances, and if this is strictly adhered to, it will definitely help individuals with an incorrect posture, to redefine and correct their ergonomic imbalance.

This area is the **"core" or tanden area** in the front of the body, about an inch below the belly button, in line with the Sacrum vertebra. This is also where the true power lies, and is the link between the grounding force beneath your feet through the core and to your upper body. This is explained in more detail further below. In a normal standing position, this is the body's center of gravity.

Re-treatment

There are many types of remedial treatment for bad posture. The main ones are Pilates, Alexander Technique, the Rolfing therapies, and Osteopathy. These are essentially teaching approaches which involve manual manipulation, neuromuscular therapy, or specific exercises, and myofascial release. I have also found that holding the basic sanchin dachi position for one to two minutes repeated three times a day, greatly relives pain in the neck, shoulders, mid-back, and low back areas.

9. Sanchin Posture in general

The sanchin posture performed regularly will relieve the tension we put on ourselves every day when we succumb to gravity and slouch. The neck is pulled in (retracted) and directly above the sternum, while the shoulders are pulled slightly back relieving pressure on the trapezius muscles, and the lumbar or small of the back is tilted slightly forward which in turn eases pressure in the small of the back and in the intervertebral discs. This then strengthens the abdominal muscles and puts the power in the core or low abdominal region. Furthermore this stance opens the mid-back and the thoracic cavity allowing you to breath more deeply. Your spine is your body's structural column with shock absorbing discs, attached to tendons and ligaments which allow only a certain amount of movement and to elastic muscles which can enhance and amplify this movement into an amazing range of motion of the entire body.

A side view of the body reveals the three natural spinal curvatures; from the neck - the cervical or inward curve; then the mid-back with an outward curve; and finally the low back or lumbar area with an inward curve. If each curve is about 35 degrees, your body's spinal column is strong, giving your head and limbs a full range of motion. During the sanchin stance the spine is kept more or less straight, and this then eases the strain on the spine and after sanchin training helps the spine to retain its natural curvature in the correct alignment. If the muscles are tight even in a relaxed state, or are weak restricting free movement, the body will then move in a an uncoordinated manner.

There are four main areas of strength and awareness in the body and if you want your body to be strong and powerful, then be consistent with your regular training, and flexible in learning to master the art of movement by using your body properly. The head and neck along with the eyes is the first area of strength and stability. The head controls all body movement and your eyes enable you to maneuver within your environment, and make you aware of your surroundings. The second area of strength and stability is the thoracic spine, which enables your upper body to twist, bend and move with the full range of motion of your arms. About an inch lower from your belly button is the center of gravity of your body and is also the area that seats the power of the whole body, from where all action and movement begins, also known as the core. This is the pelvic region of the body which contains the pelvis, lumbar spine, sacrum and the hips. Finally the feet, legs and thighs which form the base of the body and is the fourth area of strength and stability.

10. Muscular Connections

"You are only as strong as your weakest link".

The origination of all and any body maneuvers and movement is a combination of muscular motion around joints. As you perform any muscular action, there are muscles that shorten (contract) which work to move that particular part of the body. These muscles are known as *agonists.* Simultaneously there are also muscles that lengthen working to control that part of the body. These muscles are known as *antagonists*. To further enhance structural balance there are muscles that work to stabilize and hold body parts. These muscles are known as *synergists* and *fixators*. This compatible relationship between agonists, synergists, and fixators is what allows the body to move as a complete unit.

For example; here is what happens when you perform a reverse punch or gyaku-tsugi:

"Standing in zenkutsu dachi in front of the makiwara, your right arm is tucked into your chest, while your left arm is held extended in line with your face. As you continue, your achilles tendons contract to commence the beginning of your punching action. The power muscles at the front of your thighs, (quads) and the large gluteus muscles of your bottom now contract in order to speed your momentum into the hip joints delivering power to your pelvic girdle. Your abdominal muscles now stabilize your pelvis and spin in order to build up speed into the twisting action of your torso and deliver the power up into the upper back, shoulders and chest. The pull back action of your left arm increases the momentum and with the twisting action of your fist, you hit the makiwara with full force, momentum and penetration".

All this happens in a split second. Note the following:

I. *When the calf muscles shorten, the hamstring muscles lengthen in order to control the knee joints.*

II. *The muscle connection between your spine and thigh is the illiopsoas muscle and it lengthens to control your spine".*

III. *The upper back and shoulder muscles work to stabilize and control the shoulder joint for the arm to extend with speed and devastating power.*

With regular Sanchin kata training we learn to nurture and enhance this power as it uses and unites all the relevant muscle connections which unite all body areas for total body power. The floor of the dojo is used as a firm base, where forces transfer from the feet and ankle joints up the legs and into the pelvic basin. From here they send a torqueing chain reaction of forces up the torso and the core through the large muscles of the back, essentially the latissimus dorsi and the chest muscles to the shoulder joint and out through the arm. As you practice sanchin regularly you make the links throughout the whole chain stronger and stronger, ultimately making your entire body much more powerful than before. If you are weak in the upper body or the lower body sanchin training will improve these areas enhancing the uninterrupted flow of power that will give your techniques fluidity and greater strength than before.

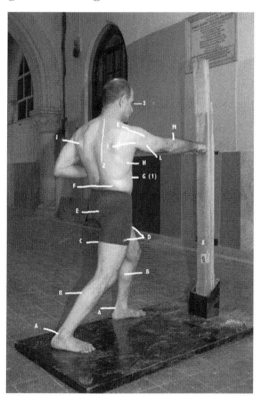

A: Achilles tendon giving pushing force from the ground, and enhancing power to the legs.

B: Calf muscles, stretching on the rear leg in an isometric contraction, with concentric contraction on the front leg.

C: Hamstrings: Act as synergists to stabilize the knee and the hip girdle.

D: Quadriceps: Contract for additional power to the pelvic and lower abdomen, the center of strength and power.(1).

E: Gluteus: Contracts to speed up power into the power center (1) 'tanden'.

F: The two oblique muscles, assist in torquing the pelvis, further accelerating the movement.

G: The lower abdomen, which includes the strength & 'tanden' (1) and the rectus and transverse abdominal muscles.

H (2): From the abdominal muscles the generated force moves upwards into the lower back as well as the thoracic center (2),

which opens outward enhancing power into the large lat muscles H.

I: For every action there is an equal and opposite reaction, Newton's third law of motion is very aptly applied here. The greater the pull back of the opposite arm, the faster and stronger the tsugi (punch).

J, K, L, M: The agonist muscles of the scapular and the rotator cuff J, now contract sending power into the deltoids K, and the triceps L, further powering the extensor muscles of the forearm M, as well as the twisting action of the fist culminates in devasting force as the first two knuckles hit the makiwara.

11. Conclusion

If you want to look good and feel good don't ever neglect the aspect of having a good posture or perfect balance. Believe me it's one of the most important factors in the long run. Bad or incorrect posture can lead to anything from a headache to constipation, to hyper acidity and these ailments are only the beginning. It can also lead to scoliosis or curvature of the spine, or a permanent hunch back. Most people want to be tall, well, just, pull in your chin, straighten those shoulders push the hips a little forward and presto you are an inch taller.

The gift of life is one to be treasured and revered, and being aware of your posture will go a long way in getting the best you want out of life.

Chapter II

Physiology of Sanchin Kata

1. Physiology of Respiration

Awake or asleep, we breathe an average of 12 to 20 times a minute, and in 24 hours we breathe in and breathe out more than 8000 liters (282 cu ft) of air. During heavy physical exercise, the breathing rate will increase considerably up to 80 times a minute. The reason for moving so much air in and out of the body is to enable the lungs to do two things: to extract the oxygen needed to sustain life and to rid the body of carbon dioxide, which is the waste product of internal chemical processes.

That breathing is essential to sustain life, is known to all humans. Most of the time the simple act of breathing is *"automatic"*, allowing input from our brain and CNS to manage the depth and rate of our breathing. However we also have the ability to change our rate and depth of our breathing consciously as do athletes, yogis and martial artists. These elite group of people have learnt the value of regulating respiration consciously, of breathing evenly and diaphragmatically, of hyperventilating for specific purposes and of suspending the breath at will.

"Without exception all experimentation with breathing must be done under the supervision of a master".

There have been instances in yoga during the practice of **"pranayama"** or breathing exercises and also in **"sanchin"** training in Karate-do where practioners have passed out and **hence** it would be wise to tread with caution.

In order to understand sanchin breathing, it is important to first understand the design of the respiratory system; and then at the way skeletal muscles draw air into lungs. Thereafter we will see the co-relation of breathing and posture and posture and breathing. We will then take a look at the physiology of respiration and examine how lung volumes and blood gases are altered in Sanchin training. Finally we will examine the practice of Sanchin breathing, in relation to all of the above.

2. The Respiratory System

The respiratory system supplies oxygen, eliminates carbon dioxide, and helps regulate the acid-base balance (pH) of the body. This system consists of the lungs, and series of passage ways leading to and from the lungs (mouth, throat, trachea, bronchi, and bronchioles).

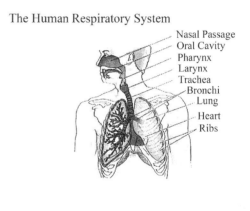

The Human Respiratory System

Nasal Passage
Oral Cavity
Pharynx
Larynx
Trachea
Bronchi
Lung
Heart
Ribs

Respiration is the overall exchange of gases (oxygen, carbon-dioxide, nitrogen) between the atmosphere, the blood and the cells.

When the body is at rest, air enters the respiratory system through the nostrils of the nose, and is warmed as it passes through a series of nasal cavities lined by mucous membrane covered with small *cilia* (small hairs) that filter out small particles. From the nasal cavity, inspired air next enters the *pharynx* (throat), which lies just posterior to the nasal and oral cavities. During sanchin breathing through partially constricted nostrils, we make use of nearly all the muscles of the throat and neck (as explained later) thereby increasing the total volume of air inhaled.

From the nasal cavities the inhaled air flows down the wind-pipe (trachea) and then divides into the right and left lungs.

The actual exchange of respiratory gases such as oxygen and carbon-dioxide between the lungs and the blood occurs at the anatomic level. It is estimated that the lungs contain 300 million alveoli that provide a very large surface area (approximately 70 square meters or 230 square feet or the size of half a tennis court) for the exchange of gases. The continuous branching of the trachea resembles a tree trunk and branches and is commonly referred to as the *bronchial tree.*

The final components of this system are the lungs, paired, cone shaped organs lying in the thoracic cavity. The right lung has three lobes; the left lung has only two. The *diaphragm* is a muscle that forms the base of the thoracic cavity, contracts during inspiration (moves downwards) and relaxes (moves upwards) to allow expiration. In sanchin breathing this muscle plays a very important role as explained below.

3. Respiratory Muscles

It is only through the action of muscular activity by the respiratory muscles that inhalation can take place. However, this is not the case during exhalation, as the lungs have the capacity to get smaller as their elasticity keeps pulling them, alongwith the rib-cage, to a smaller size. When breathing normally, three main groups of muscles are active: the *intercostal muscles, the diaphragm,* and the *abdominal muscles. However, when breathing is laboured or when the nasal passageways are constricted as during sanchin Training, the neck muscles perform the major role of inhalation.*

In sanchin breathing inhalation takes place essentially with the help of the auxiliary muscles of the neck along with the respiratory muscles.

These are the muscles of the rib-cage or to be more precise between the ribs and the diaphragm and operate simultaneously to expand and relax the chest. There are two sets of this muscle which are called the *external* and *internal intercostals*. The former do the lift and expansion of the rib-cage for inhalation, while the latter pull the ribs closer together and downwards during exhalation, more so and especially during a forced exhalation, as during sanchin kata performance.

4. The Abdominal muscles in relation to breathing

It is important to note that during breathing the abdominal muscles function mainly during deep and forced exhalations as when trying to blow up a balloon or during sanchin kata practice. Here the abdominal muscles shorten or contract, pressing the abdominal wall inward. Together with the action of the internal intercostal muscles, this forcibly decreases the size of the chest cavity with forced exhalation *except during "sanchin" practice*. As the entire body is held in an isometric contraction, there is no expansion or relaxation of the chest and /or the abdominal wall. This is what happens during the end of each action in sanchin kata or in other words during Kime. When performed correctly, all the muscles of the body become as hard as stone for that one instant of "*kime*". Throughout the performance of Sanchin Kata, the body muscles are contracted to about 80%, and only during the end of each action or at kime are the muscles contracted to as near as 100% as possible. The main focus at this point should be on the "tanden" or core area of the body. It is at this point that the abdominal wall is lifted upwards, to protect the solar plexus along with the front muscles of the neck which are also contracted to protect the trachea or the wind pipe. It is important to note here that when the head is positioned correctly, and neck muscles are contracted, the Adam's Apple or the normal protrusion of the trachea cartilage is actually pulled inwards, and along with the contracted neck muscles makes it difficult for an adversary to choke you.

5. Anatomy of the Diaphragm

Aside from surgeons and pathologists, hardly anyone ever gets to see the diaphragm, and most people have no idea of what it looks like or at best just a very basic idea of its operation in breathing.

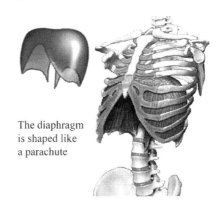

The diaphragm is shaped like a parachute

The diaphragm is a dome shaped sheet of muscle and tendon

Diaphragm

which resembles a parachute and separates the chest and abdominal areas. It is important to know that during normal and even during pressured breathing there is always movement of the thoracic cage and abdomen. This is because of the movement of the diaphragm within. In fact during sanchin training, because of the isometric contraction of the chest and abdominals, there is even greater movement of the diaphragm.

6. The Abdominal Muscles

The main function of the abdominal muscles are to protect the spine and to keep the abdominal organs in place. Sanchin training enhances and develops the abdominal structure in its entirety. Of all the muscles in the human body, during sanchin performance the most important are the muscles of the trunk, which include the major muscles associated with the spinal column and the wall of the abdomen.

Together with the action of the internal intercostal muscles, this forcibly decreases the size of the chest cavity and pushes air forcibly out of the lungs. In sanchin practice however, the chest wall is kept rigid under isometric contraction, which makes the expulsion of air more powerful. It is this air under pressure that

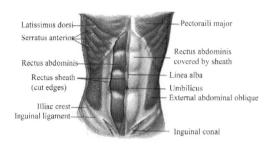

Latissimus dorsi

Serratus anterior

Rectus abdominis

Rectus sheath (cut edges)

Illiac crest

Inguinal ligament

Pectoraili major

Rectus abdominis covered by sheath

Linea alba

Umbilicus

External abdominal oblique

Inguinal conal

Abdominal Muscles

makes a sound just as when air is released from a pressure cooker. Some practitioners, when performing sanchin kata force a rasping sound, which originates more from the larynx (voice box) than from the abdomen, and this should be avoided right from the early training of this kata.

To understand this and get it right, try this out with a partner:

"Stand relaxed with feet shoulder width apart, and with your partner's palm resting on your stomach just below the belly button. Take a normal breath in and get your partner to push your stomach with medium force, keeping your mouth open. There will be a quick expulsion of air forced out through your mouth with a sound like "Haaaa". This is the sound you have to produce when training in Sanchin.

Respiration causes subtle movements of the diaphragm, which we are not normally aware of. Another technique of learning to breathe in sanchin and actually be aware of the diaphragm is to lie down on your back and place a weighted small bag just under the ribcage. On inhalation and exhalation you will be aware of the added tension that you need just simply breathing in and out. Make sure that your chest does not move, and that the weight is just enough to let your diaphragm move the weight up on inhalation and down on exhalation. This will help you to sense the involvement of the diaphragm and is an exercise to help you understand the tension needed for inhalation or concentric shortening of the muscular areas of the diaphragm and the need for controlled exhalations or eccentric lengthening of the muscular areas of the diaphragm. Remember to keep the mouth open and loose without any tension in the TMJ (temporo-mandibular joint) or jaw muscles when breathing out, and a "haaaa" sound will be heard.

7. Diaphragmatic Breathing

Professor of Anatomy in two Medical Colleges in USA, H. David Coulter and author of *"Anatomy of Hatha Yoga"* has coined the three main types of breathing as 1. abdominal- thoracic, 2. thoracic or paradoxical and 3. thoracic-diaphragmatic. In Sanchin kata breathing I have used another combination which I term as *Assisted diaphragmatic abdominal breathing.*

Abdominal - Thoracic

This form of breathing brings about a very relaxed state of mind and makes one feel very calm. Try this out: Sit on the floor in a cross legged position, with your back resting against a wall. Place your hands on your stomach and breathe in and out normally. Only the stomach should move. Count an inhalation and exhalation for 5 sec each, as 1 and do 20 repetitions. By the end of this time you will tend to feel much more relaxed.

Thoracic or Paradoxical

Breathing brings on the exact opposite effect of the above and in fact makes one feel wide awake. Sitting in a similar position as explained above, place your hands on your each side of your rib-cage, letting it expand and relax laterally and evenly like bellows. Now breathe normally in this manner for 20 breaths and see how you feel.

Thoracic - Diaphragmatic

Better known as diaphragmatic breathing and is a very natural way to breathe in normal life conditions. It brings one's attention to the middle of your body or to the borderline between the chest and the abdomen thereby creating a balance between Thoracic and abdominal breathing.

Assisted Diaphragmatic - Abdominal

This is the method to breathe, during Sanchin training. It focuses attention to your center, and it brings about the strength to keep the required tension in the abdominal muscles, which in turn brings about greater awareness of the entire back and abdominal region than any other breathing method, and greatly strengthens the core muscles better than most core training exercises.

8. Diaphragmatic breathing & psture in sanchin training

Posture and breathing go hand in glove. In fact, it's a moot statement to say whether it's "posture and breathing or breathing and posture", as one cannot be without the other. If the correct posture is not adopted during sanchin kata it would be better to stop doing this kata altogether, as this could over a period of time result in sudden cramps in the mid or low back and even in the abdominal muscles. This is because the incorrect posture will cause the wrong muscles to take the load causing an imbalance in the overall body structure, and over a period of time, this would over-develop the wrong muscles creating muscular disproportion.

Try this simple experiment: Stand in sanchin stance with your hands on your hips. Now consciously round your back, with the neck forward and try to breathe in deeply and strongly. You will find this very uncomfortable, and practically not feasible.

Now try it with the correct posture, and the breathing will be strong and smooth, with a very natural feeling. One of the best ways to attain the correct posture in sanchin kata, is with the help of a partner.

Begin by moving into sanchin dachi and have him place and hold a straight long stick on the back (along the spine), from the back of the head right down just slightly lower than your buttocks. There should be a minimum distance between the neck and the stick, and the chin should be tucked in, directly above the sternum. You should feel the stick at the back of your head, and from the start of the thoracic vertebra (mid spine) the stick should be in contact with the spine, right down till the buttocks, or the sacrum. This is the posture that should remain throughout the Sanchin Kata. In this position when you inhale and exhale, it allows fluids to flow in and out keeping the spine continually hydrated. On inhalation the spine will lengthen leading to expansion of the core. On exhalation the spine compresses as the body contracts.

Fig.1. Rounded back in Sanchin Kata is incorrect

Fig.2. Showing the straight alignment of the head and back in Sanchin Dachi.

9. The Confluence of Inhalation and Exhalation

This is one of the most crucial and important aspect of this Kata. After inhalation most practitioners tend to trap the breath in the chest instead of pushing the breath into the abdomen which makes the practitioner extremely unstable, In sanchin kata the point of the inhalation and exhalation happens first as you open into the kata, then for each of the 'tsugis' (punch) (when the fist is pulled back to the chest) and again at the end of each 'tsugi' just before the 'yoko uke' and again on completion of the 'yoko uke'. This confluence also takes place during 'nukite tsugi' and during 'Tora Guchi' actions. Nerve impulses send messages to the muscle fibers of the diaphragm even after exhalation commences and this operates to smoothen and enhance the transition between the end of each inhalation and the start of each exhalation. Imagine the breath as you feel it. On inhalation and exhalation focus on your '*tanden*' in keeping it as taught as you can.

To an outsider, viewing sanchin kata may seem very static, while in actual fact this kata and tensho are very dynamic. In any discussion on breathing, especially sanchin breathing, it is of importance to know a bit more on the **physiology** of breathing with an understanding of the volume and capacities of air in the lungs and airways at different stages of the breathing cycle during the performance of this Kata. By having this knowledge of what is happening in your body, your performance could be that much better.

10. Lung Volumes, Lung capacities, and the Anatomic Dead Space

Lung Volumes

Lung volumes consist of various volumes of air inspired (inhaled) into, and expired (exhaled) from, or contained within the lungs during breathing. There are many different ways of breathing: normally, as we do at rest, much faster when we exercise, slow and deep breathing during meditation, and sleep and many more forms as in "pranayama", (yogic breathing) and also in "ibuki", (Japanese martial arts breathing). It is now time to look more closely into the main organs of respiration - namely - the "**LUNGS**".

Human lungs are the organs of respiration. There are two lungs, with the left being divided into two lobes and the right into three lobes. Together the lungs contain about 2,400Km (1,500 mi) of airways and 300 to 500 million alveoli (tiny sacs at the end of the branches in the lungs), having a surface area about the same size as half a tennis court. Each lung weighs 2.5 pounds so the entire organ weighs about 5 pounds.

However for the sake of uniformity the medical fraternity has classified lung volumes into four categories. They are as follows:

i) Tidal volume

This is the amount of air breathed in during one inhalation or exhalation. During a relaxed state of breathing in normal adult, this amounts to about 500 ml. or 7ml/kg body weight. However this volume will dramatically change when sprinting or climbing a staircase.

ii). Inspiratory reserve volume

This is the additional amount of air that can be breathed in after a tidal inhalation, about 3,300 ml.

iii). Expiratory reserve volume

This is the additional amount of air exhaled after a normal tidal exhalation which is about 1,000 ml.

iv). Residual volume

This is the amount of air that remains in the lungs after exhaling to the very maximum, and which amounts to about 1,200 ml.

Lung capacities

The total Lung capacity depends on a person's age, height, weight, sex, and normally ranges from 4,0003 to 6,0003 cm (about 4 to 6 liters). Females tend to have a 20 to 25% less capacity than males. Tall people tend to have a larger capacity than shorter persons. Smokers (because of airway passage narrowing) may have higher residual volume due to air trapping, than non-smokers. In fact it would not be out of place to say that Sanchin training would be of great help to smokers who are in the quitting stage.

Lung capacity is also affected by altitude. People who are born and live at sea level will have a smaller capacity than those who spend their lives at a higher altitude, such as some Sherpas (a small tribe who live in the foothills of the Himalayas) who have climbed the summit of Mount Everest without the aid of oxygen cylinders.

Respiratory volumes and Capacities

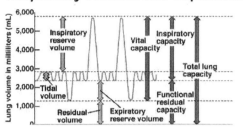

Typical resting adult respiratory rates are 10-20 breaths per minute, with 1/3rd of the breath time in inhalation. Human lungs are to a certain extent 'overbuilt' and have a tremendous reserve volume as compared to oxygen requirements when at rest. As oxygen requirements increase during exercise, a greater volume of the lungs is operfused, allowing the body to reach its carbon dioxide CO_2/ Oxygen O_2 exchange requirements. An average human breathes around 11,000 liters of air (21% of which consists of O_2) in one day.

Here now are four categories that are a combination of two or more lung volumes.

i). Vital Capacity: is the maximum amount of air a person from his lungs, after a maximum inhalation; it amounts to about 4,800 ml and is the combination of the tidal volume plus the inspiratory and expiratory reserve volumes. This is the most inclusive possible definition of the *full breath* during the actions of the tsugi, yama uke and the tora guchi techniques, in the performance of sanchin kata.

ii). Total Lung Capacity: This term is self explanatory. In a young healthy adult it amounts to about 6,000 ml and is the sum of all four lung volumes, or in other words the sum of the vital capacity and the residual volume.

iii). Inspiratory capacity: This is the total amount of air we can inhale into the lungs after a normal exhalation.

iv). Functional Residual Capacity: This amounts to about 2,200 ml and refers to the amount of air in the lungs at the end of a normal exhalation that will be mixed with a fresh inhalation. This point is very important to remember, as in Sanchin Kata all inhalations are performed with forced inhalations or pinched nose breathing. This is done to drastically reduce this value so that the fresh oxygen inhaled is mixed with a smaller volume of oxygen poor air remaining in the lungs.

Chapter III

Muscles of Respiration

1. Introduction

The various muscles of respiration aid in <u>both inspiration and expiration </u>which require changes in the pressure within the thoracic cavity. The respiratory muscles work to achieve this by changing the dimensions of the thoracic cavity.

This is extremely important, as it directly affects our understanding of the mechanics of breathing during Sanchin Kata, and is also the reason why I have termed Sanchin Breathing as "**assisted diaphragmatic-abdominal**" breathing, as mentioned earlier.

The principal muscles are the diaphragm, the inspiratory intercostals, and the expiratory intercostals, which during inhalation elevate the ribs, thus increasing the width of the thoracic cavity, which then makes the diaphragm contract (pushes downwards) to increase the

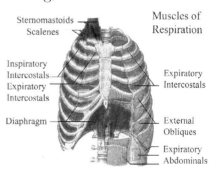

Respiratory Muscles

vertical dimensions of the thoracic cavity, and also aids in the elevation of the lower ribs.

Accessory muscles are typically used when the body needs to process energy quickly, for example during heavy exercise, during the stress response or during an asthma attack. The accessory muscles of Inspiration may also become engaged in every day breathing when a breathing disorder exists.

2. The Diaphragm

This Muscle is crucial for breathing and respiration. During inhalation the diaphragm contracts (pushes downwards), thus enlarging the thoracic cavity (the external intercostal muscles also take part in this enlargement). This reduces the intra-thoracic pressure; in other words enlarging the thoracic structure creates suction that draws air into the lungs. When the diaphragm relaxes, the air is exhaled by the elastic recoil of the lungs and tissue lining. The thoracic cavity in conjunction with the abdominal muscles also acts as an antagonist or lengthens when paired with the diaphragm's contraction. However during Sanchin kata all the muscles are kept in isometric contraction not allowing changes in either the thoracic cavity, or the abdominal cavity, which leaves only the diaphragm to descend downwards increasing the intra-abdominal pressure. This in turn allows the lifting of the abdominal wall at the end of each "kime".

Most singers and even muscians believe that the diaphragm is is the responsible muscle for a great voice. In fact, one has more control over the abdominal muscles than the actual diaphragm. The reason behind this, is that the diaphragm has relatively few proprioceptive nerve endings. However, by exercising, having good posture and balance in the rest of the body, the diaphragm naturally strengthens and works in concert with the surrounding structures, rather than in isolation.

3. The intercostal muscles

Along with the diaphragm, the intercostal muscles are one of the most important groups of respiratory muscles. These muscles are attached between each rib and are important in manipulating the width of the thoracic cage.

4. Accessory muscles of inspiration

Even in the medical fraternity, there is quite a bit of controversy as to which muscles may be considered accessory muscles of inspiration (Kendal, McCreary, Provance, Rodgers and Romani 2005).

Earlier I have termed Sanchin Breathing to be **Assisted diaphragmatic abdominal.** The main reason for having included the word *'assisted'* is because of all the various or *"auxiliary"* muscles working in concert during forced Inspiration or Inhalation.

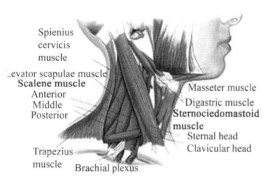

Inspiratory Muscles

These are the *sternocleomastoid* (situated in the neck and elevate the sternum), and the scalene muscles (anterior, middle and posterior). They are typically considered muscles of Inhalation.

However, other muscles on the back have also been observed to be contributing to inhalation, especially forced or partially closed nose inhalation such as the *"serratus posterior muscle"* and during forced exhalation like the *"leveators costarum"* during Sanchin kata. The scalene muscles activation coincides with the diaphragm even at rest in most humans, suggesting that it could be considered a primary muscle of respiration.

5. Anatomic dead space

This term refers to the air-filled space of the air passages, which include the nasal pathways, pharynx, larynx, trachea, right and left primary bronchi and the branches of the bronchial tree that lead to the alveoli. It is called a dead space (which totals about 150 ml) as it does not contribute to the transport of oxygen into the blood and carbon dioxide out. Medical concerns with the anatomic dead space are serious: in patients with terminal emphysema, its volume sometimes approaches and exceeds the vital capacity.

6. The abdominal muscles of expiration

In normal breathing, during expiration, the internal inter-costals depress the ribs, decreasing the chest size. The abdominal muscles pull the lower chest down, depress the lower ribs and compress the abdominal contents, which in turn exerts pressure on the chest. In sanchin kata, due to the enormous tension, the pressure created is much more and hence actually results in a type of internal massage to the organs of the chest and stomach, thus increasing the internal health of the practitioner.

7. Muscular tension in sanchin training

Here I must ask you a question:

What is the definition of a healthy muscle?

My Answer:

"The greater the disparity between its state of relaxation and contraction - the healthier the muscle".

Try this out; relax your right arm completely. Now feel your upper arm. Are the muscles soft and completely pliable like a ball of cotton wool? Or are they a bit on the tensed side? Now tighten your upper arm as in a bicep curling action and again feel your bicep muscles. Are they completely hard as the proverbial rock, or is there a small give in the bicep? Very few people can consciously achieve complete softness and total hardness. Hence in the performance of sanchin kata, all the superficial muscles must be in at

60% (beginners) and 80% (advanced) and on each of the 'kime' actions, the contraction must be pushed to 100% for that one split second and back to 60% or 80%.

At the Chief Instructors Gasshuku in Okinawa 2012, Shihan Higaonna introduced us to a Master Shiatsu expert. He astounded us with his rehabilitation techniques which were simply amazing. Sensei's who could not bend further than their knees, after his therapy were easily able to touch the floor. Others who previously had walked with a limp commenced walking straight, without any pain that they had been suffering for a very long time. Through an interpreter, he later explained that when karatekas trained hard every day their muscles tightened, became more dense and thus compressed against the corresponding bone. In short the muscles remained comparatively hard even at rest. The remedy was to ease the muscular tension through his shiatsu technique releasing the compressed muscle and making it soft and pliable. He also mentioned that he had never felt such soft muscles in an athletes body as he felt when he massaged Shihan Higaonna.

In all forms of isotonic exercise (where a movement at a joint is performed, or where tension remains unchanged whilst the muscle's length changes), exercise there are two phases of movement; the concentric phase (working against gravity as in lifting a weight) and eccentric phase (working with gravity as in setting down a weight). We know today that by keeping continuous tension (slowly lowering a weight) in the eccentric phase, we use a greater number of muscular fibers by 60-65% than by working only on concentric phase. Many students tell me quite often and very proudly that they have done 200 and more crunches, but when I make them do the same exercise correctly they barely manage 20. This is mainly because they rely on momentum, and therefor lose out completely on the eccentric phase of the crunch movement. Another way of exercising a muscle is through Isometric tension (where the muscle is kept under tension without changing the length of the muscle for a period of time). e.g. holding your leg out at full extension for a minute or two.

What this means in relation to Sanchin kata is that the muscles of the body must be kept tense at all times and never relaxed throughout the performance. Very often during the performance of Sanchin, at each step of the kata there is intermittent relaxation followed by tension. This should be avoided at all costs, especially in the hip and pelvic area.

Of all the muscles in the human body, during Sanchin performance the most important are the muscles of the trunk, which include the major muscles associated with the spinal column and the wall of the abdomen.

At this point, please allow me to digress a little and tell you a story about Hanshi Chogun Miyagi's days in the Military.

According to the book "The History of Karate" by Shihan Morio Higaonna (Sugawara Martial Arts Inc. Tokyo 1993. ISBN 0-87040-595-0) (Page 48), Sensei Chogun Miyagi was not very popular amongst his fellow soldiers due to jealousy of his tremendous strength and prowess.

In Shihan Morio Higaonna's own words:

"On another occasion, a group of men armed with bamboo and wooden swords came in the middle of the night and beat him as he lay in bed. The very next morning his attackers were shocked to see him out and running as usual. Miyagi later described how he had curled up into a ball to protect his vital areas and, using Sanchin breathing and internal power, was able to survive the attack uninjured".

In order to comprehend the above, it is essential to first understand the musculature of the Abdominal region.

You will all have probably noticed that your upper abdominal muscle are far stronger than the lower abdominal muscles, just above the pubic bone. The reason behind this is not only a question of muscular weakness, but also a question of body alignment. **The only way the transverse abdominal muscles can be contracted, and to a certain extent the lower "Rectus abdominals",**

is by tilting the pelvic joint forward which in turn activates the "illio-psoas" group of muscles intended for this purpose.

In Sanchin Kata training, I cannot stress upon you enough how very important the above fact is.

The walls of the abdominal cavity are supported entirely by the strength of the "***Rectus abdominus***" for there are no bones that provide support for this region. To make up for the lack of skeletal support, the three layers of muscles in the abdominal wall run in different directions, thus providing additional support.

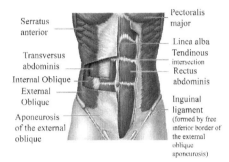

Abdominal Muscles

In Sanchin kata, the underlying purpose is to protect the internal organs by contacting the superficial muscles. A perfect example of this is the contraction of the **"external and internal oblique"** muscles which protect the kidneys when contracted (tensed). The external oblique muscle fibers run interiorly downward and toward the midline. In the second layer, the fibers of the **"internal oblique"** muscle run posterior and downward. An easy way to remember the placements of these two muscles, is to picture the fibers of the **external oblique** running in to your front pocket of your trousers, and the fibers of the **internal oblique** running diagonally into your rear pockets.

Bilateral (both sides) contraction of the internal and the external obliques compresses the abdominal cavity; these muscles are commonly activated during forced exhalation, defecation and urination.

Complete and total contraction of the entire trunk and abdominal region cannot be achieved, unless one other muscle group which encircles the abdomen like a corset is also contracted. This muscle is called the "Transversus Abdominus" muscle. Its main primary function is to compress the abdomen, support posture and help in the digestive process.

To practically understand the above paragraphs, try out this simple experiment; lie down flat on your back. Bend your knees keeping your feet on the floor about 12" from your buttocks. Keep your hands under your head in a linked position, and your elbows pointing upwards along side your head. Now raise your head and shoulders off the ground, release one hand and feel your abdomen, you will notice that only the upper rectus abdominus is tensed whilst the lower is comparatively relaxed, as are the transverse Abdominus. holding the above position.

Now, by tilting your pelvic very slightly upwards, lower the small of the back into the floor feeling your spine on the floor. Again release one hand and now feel the entire abdomen. You will notice that the lower and the upper abdominus rectus are tensed.

Now concentrate on pushing your spine still more into the ground and you will feel the oblique muscles in your back and sides coming into full contraction. Upon feeling the entire abdomen with one hand you will notice that the outer most sides or the transverse abdominus muscles are still comparatively relaxed. This emulates the 80% contraction which should be kept during Sanchin Kata. Keeping your hand on this area, make a "haaa" sound, (as when you breath out at sanchin kime) and you will now notice the total and complete contraction and compression of the trunk and the abdominal region. This is the final contraction of this region to as near as possible to 100% that is performed at the end of each kime, during the performance of Sanchin kata. One final and very important contraction is that of the anus or the sphincter muscle. This contraction completes and enhances the full contraction of the trunk and entire abdominal region.

In conclusion let me also inform you that this region is capable of tremendous conscious control vertically and even laterally, (unlike the diaphragm as discussed previously) and done in conjunction with sanchin training, will not only give you a better understanding of Sanchin kata, but will keep your internal organs in excellent health.

8. Pulling of the testicles into the abdominal cavity

As mentioned in the above story of Kanryo Higaonna Hanshi's "Saiban", we have all heard of this feat being accomplished by experts and Masters of this Kata. The main reason for this is to avoid being hurt by an opponent intent on ending any future family life.

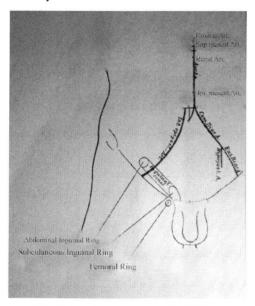

The Subculaneous Inguinal Ring

Through personal experience, and after discussing this issue with leading Doctors in the field of Urology, Anatomy, and Sex therapy, and researching on yogis, who may be capable of the same, I have come to the understanding that this technique should never be attempted without personal and direct supervision of an expert in this application. This is a highly advanced technique and could result in serious harm and injury if attempted alone.

However allow me to clarify the incorrect statement "**pulling of the testicles into the abdominal cavity**". There is **NO** place in the abdomen for the testes to go into as there is no abdominal cavity above the testicles. However the testes could be pulled into the "**superficial inguinal ring**" (subcutaneous inguinal ring) which is just under the scrotum sack or further back into the **"deep inguinal ring"** (abdominal inguinal ring). This is extremely difficult and all the Anatomy Professors and Doctors I talked with have never seen anyone actually be able to do it. This does not by any stretch of the imagination mean that it cannot be done, only that it is very difficult and should only be attempted under expert supervision.

9. Breathing in Sanchin Kata

During heavy physical exercise, the breathing rate will increase considerably up to 80 times a minutes. The reason for moving so much air in and out of the body is to enable the lungs to do two things: to extract the oxygen needed to sustain life and to rid the body of carbon dioxide, which is the waste product of internal chemical processes.

In Sanchin kata there are four basic techniques of breathing. It should be noted however that for beginners and intermediates the entire kata should be performed using method (a). It's a much simpler method and hence easier to concentrate on just one type of breathing. The emphasis for beginners and intermediates, should be on sanchin dachi, sanchin posture, and sanchin tension. It is at a higher level that the emphasis should be placed on the advanced breathing technique as described below:

a. Deep, slow and controlled inhalation, deep, slow and controlled exhalation
b. Quick inhalation, and a quick exhalation.
c. Deep and slow inhalation, and a very quick exhalation
d. Quick inhalation, and a slow and controlled exhalation.

When practicing Sensei Chogun Miyagi's Sanchin kata the emphasis is on type (a to d) breathing whereas in practicing Sensei Kanryo Higaonna's Sanchin the emphasis is on technique - type (a) . In abdominal breathing most of the work is done by the diaphragm as explained above. The ribs provide the upper parts of the cage that encloses the heart and lungs and the diaphragm forms the bottom.

In the performance of Hanshi Kanryo Higaonna's Sanchin kata you must utilise the breathing technique - type a only. As the air enters your nose you must imagine it going straight to your tan-den via the trachea and the solar plexus.

During abdominal breathing, when we breathe in, the muscular fibers of the diaphragm contract drawing the highest central part down in to the abdomen. This increases the volume of the lungs and is the essence of sanchin breathing. Once in the lung the air travels to the alveoli, where the exchange of oxygen and carbon dioxide takes place.

Like any other muscle, the diaphragm receives instructions to contract or relax from the nervous system. The nerves which supply the diaphragm are called the **"phrenic nerves"**. These nerves originate from the cervical vertebrae (3rd.- 5th.) of the spinal column), and passes down into the lungs and heart to reach the diaphragm. For karate instructors this is of vital importance. In fact the chu-dan tsugi applied in **Sanchin** kata and in other katas as well is aimed at the phrenic nerve plexus which is situated about one inch below the right and left nipple. In women an *ippon-ken* (single knuckle punch) on this point can be as devastating as a kick in the groin for men. In Karate terminology this attack point is called "ganka".

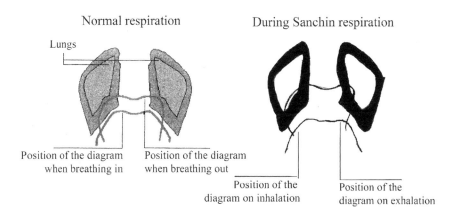

Normal respiration   During Sanchin respiration

Lungs

Position of the diagram when breathing in   Position of the diagram when breathing out

Position of the diagram on inhalation   Position of the diagram on exhalation

In 1987 I had undertaken a research study under Dr. Cherian Verghese (M. D. D. P. M, Dr. Shubha S. Thatte(Ph.D.) and Dr.

D. R. Doongaji M. D. , M. S. , F. R. C., D. P. M. at the K. E. M. Hospital and G. S. Medical College Bombay. This study was a psychological assessment of 72 karate students at various levels of training as compared to practitioners of other contact and non-contact sports.

The main focus of this study was to find out the levels of aggressiveness and anger at various levels of training between karatekas and other contact and non-contact sports.

The following closing paragraph of the study gives us the answer:

"*The Black Belts, it seems, are better adjusted individuals than Athletes and Boxers. Though the subjects in this study are psychiatrically normal, it is possible that even disturbed persons could benefit from this ancient practice of Karate-do*".

In Sanchin the **kime** is of utmost importance. At each **kime** point **ALL** the breath must be forced out and held for at least a second. What happens physiologically is, to say the least quite interesting. On the exhalation, the carbon dioxide is washed out, which trains the lungs to exchange Oxygen more efficiently. This in turn, has a therapeutic effect on the **neurotransmitters** in the brain. In the following explanation of the **ENDOCRINE** system I will explain this in more detail.

In the course of the afore-mentioned study, between contact and athletic sports and Karate, the Black Belts were found to be the least aggressive from all others. I personally attribute this to regular disciplined Karate training in general and to regular Sanchin training in particular. As mentioned earlier, the breathing in and out under constant pressure, has a calming effect of neurotransmitters in the "**hypothalamus**" area of the brain.

After many years of Sanchin training, these chemical messengers, **serotonin, dopamine, glutamate, and endorphins,** which enter the blood stream directly would leave the practioners experiencing tranquility and peace of mind.

10. The Vital Force - KI

Eastern philosophy has always maintained the theory of vital force that permeates through every living cell of our bodies. They also state that there are zones or meridians or channels of energy that traverse throughout the body, linking organs and other body parts. It is also stated that through the daily practice of Sanchin kata we can gain phenomenal power of this vital force. Hence I have thought it necessary to include this fascinating phenomenon of energy.

All of us are an expression of energy which permeates all living organisms. Because we cannot perceive energy with our eyes, it does not mean it does not exist. In both, Chinese and Ayurvedic medicine, health is seen as the flowing and harmonious movement of energies at subtle levels. In the east this energy has various names. In India we call it **"prana"** to the Tibetan Lamas it is **"lung-gom"**. It is known as **"sakia tundra"** or **"ki"** to the Japanese Shinto priests as well as to all martial artists. The Chinese call it **"ch'i"**. In the west it is loosely translated as **"vital energy,"** **"vital force"**, or **"life-force"**.

It is not surprising then to note that all the Martial arts of the East have one form or another of breathing techniques integrated into their systems. In **"Kalarypyatt"** there are more than 5 forms of breathing. **"Arnis and Kali"** which are the martial arts of the Philippines have two to three breathing forms depending on each style of the art. **"Te-kuan-do"** of Korea has two breathing forms, and practically each style of the Chinese mainland, has its own form of Sanchin. Nearly all the martial arts of Japan from have some form of breathing technique incorporated in their styles. **"Ki", Ch'i, or Prana"**, is difficult to explain and even more so to understand.

Through the genius of **Albert Einstein** we have come to understand the nature of the known universe. All matter and even anti matter is made up of some form of vibration. Light, sound, gravity are all vibrations oscillating at different frequencies." **Vital energy"** represents some form of electricity. This does not mean it is electricity, but that its behavior, responses and reactions indicate that many of the laws applying to electricity also apply to **vital energy.** This energy is considered as having clearly distinct and established pathways, definite direction of flow, and characteristic behavior as well-defined as any other circulation system such as blood and the vascular system.

The movement of this energy is based on two opposing fields or "polarity". We term this polarity as "Positive and Negative" forces. In China, it is referred to as **"Yin and Yang".** The best explanation of these two forces I have read, comes from **"Ted Kaptchuk"** in his book *"The Web That Has No Weaver":*

"Yin-Yang theory is based on the philosophical construct of two polar complements, called Ying and Yang. These complementary opposites are neither forces nor material entities. Nor are they mythical concepts that transcend rationality. Rather, they are convenient labels used to describe how things function in relation to others and to the universe. They are used to explain the continuous process of natural change".

We are all aware of the scientific fact that at the **"molecular"** level all living and non-living matter is made up of chemical substances that are collections of atoms. All atoms consists of protons (+ly charged), neutrons (no charge) and electrons (-ly charged). Thus at the atomic level the body is a mass of energy fields all influencing each other. The Chinese do not however, think of elements as we do, as separate individual static things. They conceive them as beings acting according to their nature; water is always flowing, dissolving, nourishing, or extinguishing, and each of the other elements (earth, fire and wood) is active according to its nature.

In Chinese thought there are two progressions of elements: one in which each grows out of the other; and the opposite, in which each defeats the next in turn.

Furthermore, certain qualities such as strength and weakness, resisting and yielding, going forth and returning, and so on, were isolated as being fundamental attributes of all living matter, and were especially related to human existence .

As Lao Tzu Wrote:

'Man when living is soft and tender; when dead he is hard and tough. All animals and plants when living are tender and fragile; when dead they become withered and dry. Therefore it is said: the hard and tough are parts of death; the soft and tender are parts of life. This is the reason why the soldiers when they are too tough cannot carry the day; the tree when it is too tough will break. The position of the strong and great is low, and the position of the weak and tender is high.

Chapter IV

Actions of Sanchin Kata

1. Mukso "No Mind"

In most traditional style of Karate-do, "mukso" is the command given at the beginning and end of every session to ready the participants to either get their minds in gear for the session or to re-play the session in their minds to the mistakes and the encouragement that may have been pointed out during the session, and on what to improve upon in their next class.

Literally mukso may mean meditation and / or concentration, but from a practical point of view it may also refer to a state of mind which is free and un-cluttered. In the dojo when the command of mukso is given by the senior most student, the eyes are closed and the mind is calmed through a 1:2 abdominal breathing cycle. Make sure that there is no movement of the chest during inhalation or exhalation, as only the abdomen should be allowed to inflate and deflate. Now breath in for 3 seconds and out for 6 seconds, without holding the breath at any time. Do this for twenty breaths. Within this period of time your mind will clear itself, both in the beginning of the session and at the end. The command mukso yamae ends this time of meditation and students open their eyes.

2. Kamae(構え) - On Guard

Whilst this word roughly translates to "posture", in Japanese Martial Arts it refers to a position of readiness pre-paratory to an attack or defense. The Kanji of this word means 'base'.

Kamae is to be differentiated from the word "tachi" which means 'stance' pronounced "dachi" refers to the position of the body from the waist down, Kamae refers to the posture of the entire body, as well as encompass-ing one's mental posture or in other words one's attitude. These connected mental and physical aspects of readi-ness may be referred to individually as kokoro-kamae and mi-kamae.

In traditional Okinawan Goju Ryu Karate-do, there are many 'on-guard' postures or positions. For example chudan morote no kamae (middle body on guard position); jo-dan no kamae or (Upper body on guard position); ge dan no kamae or (lower body on guard position) and others.

One of the most fundamental on guard position is the "yoi no kamae" used at the beginning and end of every kata. It is interest-ing to note that while most Goju styles have the arms at the side in yoi no kamae at the beginning and end of all kata, the adherents of Sensei Chogun Miyagi, cross the left hand over the right at the groin level standing in the closed heel stance or musubi dachi, since he had invented this position after many years of research*.

In any confrontation an aggressive or threatening pose is an invitation to disaster. First of all this would indicate that anger has taken over and would override and impede the body's learnt response from karate training. But with a yoi no kamae, you project a non threatening posture while at the same time protecting your most vulnerable area "your groin". Furthermore, this position will also allow for an instant response of defense and counter attack, should it be called for, thanks to the thousands of repetitions of all the katas learnt as all Katas begin from Yoi No Kamae. (* History of Karate by M Higaonna).

3. Tako ashi sanchin dachi & musculature of the lower body

Sanchin Dachi with the gripping action of the toes (Tako Ashi)

From the beginning of Sanchin kata and throughout its performance the correct positioning of the feet and their constant tension in gripping the floor is of primary importance. In fact this action is called "Tako ashi" in Japanese, meaning Octopus stance. Try to create a feeling of suction between the soles of your feet and the floor. Then spread your toes with a inward pulling action of the toes to grip the floor even tighter. This is brought about by the muscles of the *"anterior tibial compartment"* or the front leg muscles which allow these muscles to contract and in turn extend the toes and flex the ankle joint.

Concentrate your tension on your "*Achilles tendon*" which should be hard as wood and in wards on the calf muscles or "*gastronemius*" and the "*soleus*" muscles. The thigh muscles are turned outwards thereby turning the "*vastus medialious*" or inner thigh muscle outward. By this action, these muscles form a wedge, which prevents an opponent's "ge-dan geri" or groin kick to reach its intended target.

One of the most important muscles in the lower extremity and unfortunately often ignored are the gluteal or more often referred to as the "*butt*" muscles which are in fact three muscles with the largest forming the roundness of the buttocks and called appropriately "*gluteus maximus*", and the other two are called "*gluteus medius*" and "*gluteus minimus*". All three muscles originate at the top of the pelvic bone near the base of the spine, but the gluteus maximus crosses over the other two muscles and ends in the rear of the femur bone, whereas the gluteus medius and minimus end in the side of the femur bone.

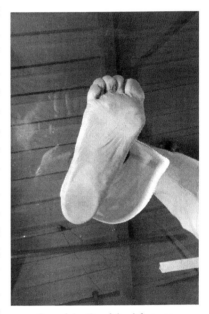

Sanchin Dachi with toes lifted, before gripping.

These three gluteal muscles stabilize the trunk and the thighs, and by acting together enable functional movement of the body. Together the three muscles stabilize the pelvis by balancing the femur bone in the upper leg. When you run you fully activate the gluteus maximus which serves to control the flexion of the trunk and hip muscles, extend the thigh muscle and decelerate the swing leg.

Quite often when people join our class at a late age, or after leading a sedentary life style, they complain within a month of training of low back and hip pain. On assessing their lower muscle strength, I have found one of two types of problems. Most com-

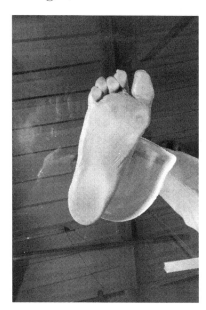

monly their gluteal muscles are very weak which renders them powerless to carry out their stabilizing function. As a result, the hip flexor muscle which run from the pelvis to the lower back bears the burden of stabilizing the body instead. When the hip flexor muscles place the strain and stress on the vertebrae in the lower spine, it results in pain in the lower back.

In second instance, I have found that the quadriceps muscles are over developed, and these muscles take over the work of the weaker hamstring and gluteal muscles, thus, once again creating an imbalance which again results in low back pain.

Sanchin Dachi with toes gripping

Sanchin kata training and even the practice of sanchin dachi helps in strengthening the gluteals to a very large extent, and over time results in no pain in the low back and hip areas. The lifting of the pelvis, and the consequent torque and tension in the low abdomen (core) enhances the stabilizing effect of the gluteal muscles and relaxes the tension in the low back or lumbar area in the spine. Thus it is important that the pelvic tilt is not relaxed during the entire performance of the kata. For juniors and seniors alike, it is important to keep the anus muscles also locked throughout the performance of this kata.

4. Movement forward & backward

General

Sanchin dachi or the sanchin stance is often called the hour glass stance, and I presume that the reasoning behind this is the inward position of the feet resemble the two upturned and down-turned hour glass containers. Be that as it may, the movement in sanchin both forward and backward is crescent shaped. In this way the body keeps the center of gravity centered and constant about two inches below the navel. Thus, there is no loss of balance as the whole body moves as one unit, unlike normal stepping or walking, either forward or backward. Here, it is important to remember that the founder of Goju Ryu, Hanshi Chogun Miyagi would start teaching beginning students Sanchin Kata, before any other kata. Once a student has more or less perfected his forward and backward movement in sanchin dachi, he is better able to grasp and understand the concept of whole body movement in any other stance. It is equally important to note that there should be little or zero sideway shifting or tilting of the body when moving forward or backward, and this not only keeps the body in perfect balance but also avoids telegraphing your intention to your opponent.

Starting from musubi dachi (heels together and feet pointing outwards at about 45°) with hands on waist or obi, the feet join together in hai soku dachi. The head should be tucked in, with the eyes gazing straight ahead. As far as possible avoid looking at your feet to see if your stance or movement is correct or not, as this bad habit will always ruin your technique and stance. Instead do your techniques in front of a mirror. Remember the position of the head controls the body. Try this simple test:

"Stand with feet about shoulder width apart. Keep your head straight, and ask your partner to gently push you with just two fingers at the center of your sternum. He will find it a bit difficult to push you backward. The second time around, tilt your head as far back as possible looking up at the ceiling. Now ask your partner to push you backward again. You will lose your balance instantly".

In self defense one of the sure-fire ways to throw an opponent is to tilt his head in the direction of your throw. This may not be allowed in Judo, but in a life or death situation, anything goes. Looking at your own feet to check your stance at any time and especially during kata practice should be avoided completely.

After retracting the head inwards, the chin should be pointing down in line with the sternum. The lower stomach should be pulled in slightly, and the pelvis tilted forward. The knees should be slightly bent. Keeping the weight on the right foot slightly, make a outward crescent

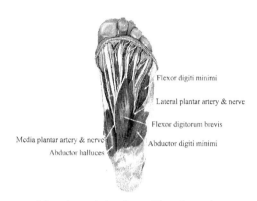

Flexor digiti minimi

Lateral plantar artery & nerve

Flexor digitorum brevis

Media plantar artery & nerve

Abductor digiti minimi

Abductor halluces

Muscles of the foot (first Layer)

movement with the right leg keeping the tension on the inside of the foot (abductor hallicus tendon & muscle), as well as the leg (the calf or the gastrocnemius muscle), until reaching the correct width of the sanchin step. At this point of time, turn the leading foot and the rear foot slightly inwards, and transfer the weight of the body initially on center of the feet (pressing the flexor digitorium brevis muscle) as if trying to create a suction type action and then onto the outer edge of the feet (lateral planter muscle). Now spread out the toes and grip the floor as if taking root contracting all the muscles and tendons of both feet. Keep the pressure on all the toes, especially the little toe, as the Abductor muscle of the little toe is the controlling muscle to help in lifting and fixing the arch of the foot. The muscular tension should be felt through the feet, inwards in the legs, and outwards in the thighs (inner thigh muscles), and pelvic girdle. It should be centered here at the tanden point (about two inches below the navel and opposite to the sacrum vertebra) and radiated out into the upper body. Now repeat the action of moving forward with the rear leg keeping the foot always in contact with the floor. Do ten to twenty steps forward. When moving backward, straighten the inward angle of the leading foot, and keeping the foot and heel in contact with the floor perform the semi circular step backward. On completion turn both feet slightly inwards in sanchin dachi. At no point release the tension totally in the feet, legs, thighs pelvic girdle and the upper body. Remember to keep the same distance in the backward step as in the forwards step. Do ten to twenty steps backwards. Keep practising sanchin stepping every day.

Muscles of the Legs

The thighs have some of the strongest muscles in the human body, the front muscles or the rectus femoris muscles, also known as the quads or quadriceps, and the longest muscle of the human body, the adductor longus, as well as the inner thigh muscles the vastus medalis, the outer thigh or vastus lateralis,

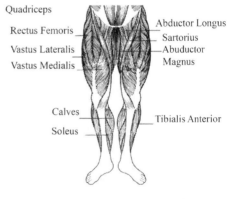

Anterior (front) leg muscles

and equally importantly the back of the thigh or the bicep femoris also known as the hamstring muscles.

Our founder, Sensei Chogun Miyagi, having undergone medical training, probably knew that underdeveloped hamstrings could sooner or later create problems in the knee joint and or the lumbar spine if it was not at least 80% as strong as the Quadricep muscles, and possibly could have been one of the reasons of his changing the kata to moving backwards instead of keeping the original turning around movement.

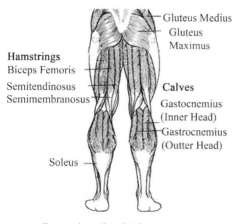

Gluteus Medius
Gluteus Maximus

Hamstrings
Biceps Femoris
Semitendinosus
Semimembranosus

Calves
Gastocnemius (Inner Head)
Gastrocnemius (Outter Head)

Soleus

Posterior (back) leg muscles

When we move forward, we are constantly contracting and thus strengthening the front of the thigh muscles, while the back of the thigh muscles act as stabilizers and antagonistic muscles. When we move backward we contract the back of the thigh muscles and strengthen them.

At various points in my teaching career, I have tried to test certain theories, mostly to find out what works and what doesn't. I once tried out an experiment to see the importance of sanchin dachi training. I selected a group of juniors who had just joined and started them on sanchin dachi training every session for the next three months along with all the other basic actions and techniques. I did the same with another group of juniors who had joined six months later, but without specifically concentrating on sanchin dachi. What I suspected was quite true. The first group learnt their geri waza (kicking techniques) very much faster than the second group, including yoko geri (side kick), and mawashi geri (circular kick). Even their upper body techniques had much more power. Do note that this was by no means a strict scientific study but more of a observation of sorts.

The abdominopelvic connection

As the term above implies, it covers all the abdominal, back and hip muscles, and when used the way it should be used, this area becomes the core or the generator of power of the human body. Remember an inch or two, below the navel, opposite where the sacrum is situated, is the center of gravity as well as the center of your power (*tanden'*). Furthermore, when a person has developed and strengthened this area, he becomes strong all over and now has the ability to deliver real strength and power in his actions and movements.

Watching two judokas during *'randori'* or free sparring you will notice when one contestant tries a front throw, his opponent will instinctively lower his hips thus centering himself and preventing himself from being thrown. We instinctively tighten our abdomen when we

Normal Spine   Lordosis of the Spine

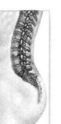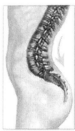

Exaggerated Lumbar Curve

Normal spine and Lordosis/ exaggerated lumbar curve

are about to fall or slip, which helps us to relocate our center. This is also the area where forces are absorbed and transferred, sometimes very quickly as during a free sparring session, and sometimes slowly during the performance of Kata Sanchin and Tensho.

The Pelvis is the area where all action is torqued and counter balanced. For example, in a straight right hand punch where the right leg and hand are forward, the pelvic or hip initially twists to the left and then torqued to right at the point of impact increasing stability and avoiding over extension of the punching arm. Whereas in a reverse punch where the right hand is used with the right leg behind and the left leg in front, the hip or pelvis is directly torqued in one direction only, namely to the left, as in the case of a right hand reverse punch maximizing power at the point of impact.

Mostly due to an incorrect posture, people complain of pain in the low back or lumbar area. This could happen due to an increased lumbar curve or *'Lordosis"* or even due to a flattening of this natural curve known as the Flat back syndrome. If it is the former, then stretch the *'psoas'* muscle (*lie down on a bed or table with one leg off the bed and towards the floor and the other bent and tucked in towards your chest*) and strengthen the lower abdominal muscles (*leg raises*). If it is the latter then stretch the hamstring muscles (*extend one leg on a small stool or stair and keeping the back straight lean forward and touch your toes)* and strengthen the low back muscles (*back extensions on a fit ball or roman chair).* Learn to keep your natural curve in this area. Remember that in the last two vertebra of the lumbar spine and the first vertebra of the sacrum is where the spine moves in two different directions at the same time, making it a potential weak area. Practise walking in Sanchin Dachi forward and backward to strengthen this area.

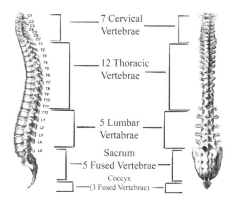

7 Cervical Vertebrae

12 Thoracic Vertebrae

5 Lumbar Vertabrae

Sacrum
5 Fused Vertebrae
Coccyx
(3 Fused Vertebrae)

Spinal Column lateral and posterior views

Correct Spinal Posture in Sanchin Kata

THE SPINE - NECK TO BASE

The spinal column is quite literally a masterpiece of body architecture. It is the cornerstone of support and even the slightest malfunction can affect any and / or all body areas including the organs and extremities. As mentioned earlier, Sanchin and Tensho Katas could help in correcting bad posture and also in rehabilitation from injuries, and in increasing the muscularity of the back and core. I speak from personal experience.

MUSCULATURE OF THE BACK

This I know is due to over 30 years of Judo on mats placed on concrete flooring along with quite a few motorcycle and other accidents. The fact that I still am able to train and teach is thanks only to the shape my muscles are in and to a large extent to my regular training in our breathing katas. In fact every time the pain gets intense, I practice standing in sanchin dachi for a minute or two, and the pain gradually releases. I was told to practise this by Shihan Higaonna, and he also mentioned that holding the sanchin posture had helped Sensei Terrauchi from low back pain also.

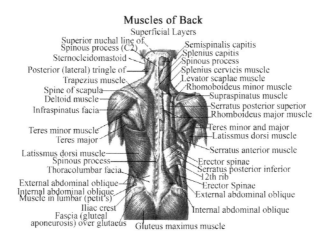

Muscles of Back
Superficial Layers

Today, most people spend a lot of time sitting in front of computers, with hunched shoulders and a drooping neck. Sitting more than 60 minutes at a time day after day, for a year or more, could result in anything from a severe muscular strain to even a slipped disk, not only in the cervical or neck area but anywhere along the spine and especially in the Lumbar area or low back. This problem of bad 'posture' is not only for the sedentary, unfortunate but true, it is seen in people active in sports too especially in the area of bodybuilding. Most amateur bodybuilders, workout what they see in the mirror, and not putting in the same time and effort in working out on what they don't see. By working out on the chest and arms only, they neglect to a large extent their back and scapularis muscles, and in time develop hunching shoulders and a forward neck. This eventually will lead to pain in the neck, traps, and even cervical spondylosis.

Most athletes know that they have to include strengthening workouts for their deltoids (all three heads), latissimus dorsi, major pectoralis, upper traps, and the rectus abdominal muscles. However, what is ignored is the imbalance that can develop between the front of the shoulder and back. When the large chest muscles(pectoralis major) and latissimus (Lats or wings) are overdeveloped in relation to the lower trapezius, rhomboids and posterior deltoids (upper back and rear shoulder muscles) imbalance occurs and injuries are just waiting to happen.

Sanchin training can greatly correct this imbalance. Just prior to the commencement of the Kata, gently pull the inner borders of your scapula (shoulder blades) inwards and downwards with the least effort and hold this position until the command of "Yoi". This is a very slight and subtle action, and at the same time gently retract the neck inwards, until your chin is just above the sternum. Focus on bringing together and pushing down the shoulder blades just a bit in the morote chudan uke, the chudan tsugi, the nukite tsugi and during the tora guchi actions as well. During all these actions the pectoralis, lats, and the abdominal muscles should be contracted at the completion of their actions.

Remember that the "*rotator cuff*" muscles are dependent on the correct positioning of the shoulder blades for strong power as well as effective control. If the shoulder blade is angled or pushed outward, for example during the tsugi (punch) action, it will be very weak and your hand will be very easy to be pushed in any direction. This will also offset your balance either forward or backward. A very slight pull or push from the back will easily upset your balance and the sanchin stance as well.

As you begin the kata from the 'yoi' position keep the following points in mind:

1. *Make a tight fist commencing from the little finger to the first finger and thumb. This will contract the flexors and extensors of the forearm.*

2. *Keep the contact and pressure on both your forearms as you move into the two hand chudan uke. This pressure will contract the*

minor and major muscles of your chest, scapularis, and the rotator cuff muscles. Do not engage the head of the trapezius muscle, rather focus on the body and tail end of these muscles. (see diagram of back musculature above).

3. *As you complete this position, bring your focus onto your Lat muscles.*

4. *Moving onto the next action of pulling back your hand bring your mind onto your Scapularis (shoulder blade) muscles. (See diagram of back musculature).*

5. *As you begin the tsugi (punching) action turn your wrist to a pronated (thumb pointing to the ground) position, and keep the inside of your punching hand forearm in full contact with that side of your body.*

6. *Midway through the punch and as the punching arm extends, focus on your lats and the pectoral muscles.*

7. *As you complete the tsugi, twist your wrist very slightly for the 'kime' action contracting your triceps and all the muscles described above.*

8. *Finally as you perform the chudan uke kamae, bring back your focus on your lat and scapularis and bicep muscles. Needless to mention, all the muscles of your abdominals including the obliques, should be in tension throughout the performance with concentration on the tanden.*

9. *As you move onto the 'nukite tsugi' bring your focus onto all the muscles you used during the tsugi movements, and at the 'kime' action concentrate on the pectoral, lats and equally important the lower abdominal muscles.*

10. *At the commencement of the 'tora guchi' focus on the inside of your chest of the upper hand and the outside of your chest of the lower hand.*

11. *As you complete the two hand circular action of the 'tora guchi', bring your concentration to squeezing the shoulder blades and on keeping your shoulders down. There should be no lifting of the shoulders.*

12. *As you bring the arms forward in the punching action of 'tora gu-chi', bring your mind back to the muscles used in your tsugi actions.*

13. *Most importantly keep the neck straight, the shoulders down and pelvic tilt constant throughout the kata.*

ATLAS SHRUGGED - THE SHOULDERS

One of the most important aspects of Sanchin Kata is the nearly straight alignment of the neck, back and pelvis. Normally when one is in the natural upright position, there are four curvatures; first in the cervical area, and second in the thoracic, the third in the Lumbar and the fourth in the Sacrum.

In Sanchin dachi however, as you take the stance, the pelvis is turned forward which as explained earlier tenses the lower **rectus abdominus** muscles as well as the external and internal oblique muscles. At the same time the chin is pulled slightly inwards, which in turn straightens out the back of the neck or the upper cervical vertebrae and aligns it with the upper and mid back area. This action also tenses and strengthens the "**sternomastoid**" muscles of the neck. With regular training in "**hojo-undo**" these muscles can be strengthened to the point where even a two handed choke hold becomes ineffective.

For the maximum amount of "**muscular contraction**" to be maintained during all the actions of blocking and punching, focus your mind on the "**teres major, teres minor and latissimus dorsi muscles**". These muscles are situated just below the armpit in your back, and the "lats" on contraction can be made to flare outwards like a bat's wings. Even advanced students often get this action wrong. This is because they put their concentration on the trapezius muscles, shoulders or arms. If counter resistance is given to the punching or blocking arms and if the concentration and focus is kept on the shoulders or arms, It becomes extremely difficult for the practitioner to maintain the muscular endurance in his blocking and punching actions. Another important point of focus is to keep the scapulae of the shoulder blades completely flat, in line with the rest of the upper back. If the shoulder blades poke outwards (posteriorly) it makes the entire shoulder girdle weak, and makes it even harder to maintain the constant strength in blocking and punching movements.

In the punching and blocking actions, the fist must be held as tight as possible, and without release. In the open hand actions the palm must be stretched and tight with the thumb locked into the palm.

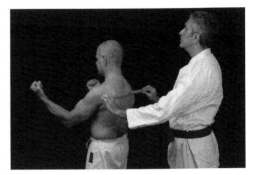

Flat Shoulder blades
(Correct position)

At the end of each blocking action when **"kime"** is performed, the contraction is focused on the **"biceps brachii"** and at the **"kime"** of each punching action contract all arm muscles and the **muscles of the chest** as well.

Another important factor to keep in mind is to have the punching arm in contact with the side of the body when pulling back the arm and also when extending it forward for the punching action. When the arm is in contact with the body during the pull back movement in preparation for the next punching action, it contracts the **'teres major and minor muscles'** which in turn help in stabilizing the shoulder blades.

Now during the punching action if the arm is **not** brushing against the body upto the elbow joint, you will only be using the joint of the arm and shoulder with very little help from the major punching muscles which are the chest and the Lats. It will also contract the **'serratus anterior'** muscles, or the arrow head shaped muscles at the side of the rib cage, easily seen during a pull up in a well defined body.

A further detailed note on these muscles is of importance as this muscle group is sometimes referred to as "*the big swing muscle*"

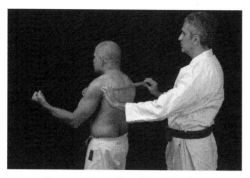

Protruding shoulder blades
(Incorrect position)

or *"boxer's muscle"*. So why is it called the *'boxer's muscle'?* Because it is largely responsible for the protraction of the scapula, or in other words, the pulling of the scapula forward and around the rib cage that occurs when a punch is executed.

The Arms – be ready - block – be ready – attack.

On Guard Defense

Attack

The Arms and legs are the instruments of attack and defense, within the symphony of the body during any and all physical confrontations. From the beginning of Sanchin Kata to the end the arms are in constant tension and movement.

At the '**YOI**' position, the thumbs of both hands are bent inwards along the palms, thanks to the remarkable *"hinge joint'* of the thumb and the *'adductor muscle'*. The hinge joint is truly unique since it allows for an extraordinary range of movement. The combination of these different movements enables the thumb to extend across the palm and to the fingers. The opposable thumb is found only in humans.

As the arms cross each other the fingers start to close and this action of making a fist should start from the little finger *(which uses the Extensor digitorium muscle)* onto the other fingers. The making of a fist should begin by bending the fingers one after the other from the second knuckle joint onto the top of the palm, and then to the first joint towards the palm. At this point the thumbs lock over the first two fingers, and should stay locked until the open hand movements commence.

I often see students during the performance of kihon kata (Basic actions) and Sanchin kata during the punching actions, opening and closing their fists time and again. This should be avoided, as it will relax and tense the arm muscles and thus loose out in power and focus.

As the arms cross move into *'morote chudan kamae', or two hand mid level on guard position*. The elbow should be one fist width from the body, with the fists about an inch or two below the shoulders. At the end of the uke action, twist the wrist slightly outwards, as this will further contract the *'biceps'* as well as the minor and major chest and also the upper and mid back muscles.

Allow me a small digression here. The *'chudan Uke'* movement is one of the first actions we learn, and yet it is also the one action that is least used in free sparring. This is probably because trying to do this action in its basic form is quite cumbersome and hence not used. In free sparring when we punch we do not use a classic *'oi tsugi'*, but rather a variation of it by using a kizami tsugi or a gyaku tsugi. Similarly if you want to really use an effective chudan uke, use your lead hand to deflect the opponents punch then just turn your wrist outward with your back hand which will block the on coming punch just like a chudan uke, this action leaves your front hand free to use as kizami tsugi instantaneously.

Now back to Sanchin kata. In the pull back just prior to the execution of the punch, keep your inner forearm in contact with the side of your body and just as your inhalation ends and exhalation begins, start turning your wrist using both the extensors and flexors of the forearm. At the end of the punch focus on the first two knuckles with just a very slight twist of the wrist. At this point do not forget to retain the tension in the chudan uke arm, keeping the scapula flat and the rotator cuff muscles contracted. Also note that the shoulder blade should be flat during all actions of the arms, and should not protrude as this will de-stabilize and weaken your tsugi and uke movements.

During the open hand movements of '*nukite tsugi*' open the fist, but keep the thumb tight against the palm, contracting the diagonal part of '*adductor pollicis*' muscle - the fleshy muscle just underneath the thumb.

In the Tora Guchi movements, remember to keep the thumbs as tight as possible across the palms, and in the double hand pushing action focus on the heels of both palms as they will contact the opponent.

Open Hand - The Defending Attack

The '*Nukite Tsugi* or '*Spear Hand*' can be used in a vertical (as in Sisochin Kata) or in the horizontal position as in Sanchin Kata. In both these applications it is the muscles of the chest and lats as the main power muscles whilst the rotator cuff muscles act as the synergists and the abdominal wall as the stabilizers. I have named it as a defending attack as it can be used by one hand to block an opponents punch or kick while the other hand can simultaneously attack using a variety of techniques such as: '*Nukite*' (spear hand); '*Haito uchi*' (ridge hand strike); and '*Shuto*

Uchi' (knife hand strike). The blocking hand can also be used in attacking immediately after the blocking action, using the attacking limb as a springboard to deflect and instantly attack. The blocking and deflection can be done with either the back (dorsal aspect) or the palm of the hand.

The Tiger's Mouth – Tora Guchi

If "Sanchin Kata" is refereed to as the **hallmark** of Okinawan Goju Ryu in general and IOGKF in particular, then most definitely the **"tora guchi"** is the **"torch bearer"** of the style.

In some Katas the complete movement of this action is performed: Gek sai dai Ni; Sanchin; Tensho and Superimpei, whereas in others a variant form of this action is used, e.g.: Gek Sai Dai Ich; Saipha; Seiyunchin; Sisochin; Sanseru; Serpai; Krunpha; and Seisan.

The literal translation of *"tora guchi"* is *"tiger's mouth"* and the movement of the hands complements the vision of a Tiger biting down on his victim.

During the performance of 'tora guchi' the action is done in its entirety defining its grace, and at the same time strength and power and above all its fluidity, but for the sake of its underlying history and its secrets of **"MUDRA"** or hand signs I will break it into its THREE distinct parts.

Tora Guchi' begins with one hand bent at the elbow with the open palm facing inwards and the other hand across the body with the palm facing towards the ground, and the top hand elbow lightly touching the down turned palm. In Bharat

Natyam and Kathak (the age-old dance forms of India) this *'mu-dra' is* called *"abhaya - vardan mudra"*, where *'abhaya'* represents protection and dispelling of fear while *'vardan'* signifies the giving, compassion and granting a favour.

Left: Picture of Nataraj in the dance of Creation. Right: Picture of wood carving of the Karate Deity *"Busaganashi"*.

Also note the similarities in the two photos above, and one wonders the real connection between these two "Deities" from the two corners of the world.

The simultaneous circling action of both arms ending with both arms pulled back in line with the chest, with one palm and fingers pointing upwards and other downwards, (the second part of tora guchi) represents according to **"Tantric Yoga"** the opening of knowledge or the awakening of the two sleeping serpents the **"kundalini"** - the first **"chakra"** of the body.

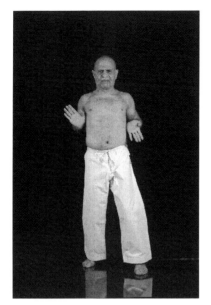

Actions of Tora Guchi

The third part is the pushing of the two hands forward represents the dispelling of fear and ignorance and awakening to the
truth and knowledge.

From the realm of mythology and history, let's get back to prac-
ticality. In the beginning of tora guchi, focus on the biceps of the
upper and lower hand and the chest muscles on both sides as well
as on the lats, keeping the shoulders down and not engaging the
head of the traps and most importantly keeping the palms as tight
as possible with full pressure on the thumbs of both hands. As
the simultaneous circling of both hands begins, breathe in deeply
through the nose forcing the breath deep into the lower tanden
or stomach, keeping the forearm in contact until the palms are
drawn back on either sides of the chest, with one palm pointing
upwards (Jodan) and the other downwards (gedan). Now breathe
out forcefully and at the same time push the arms in front until
they are nearly straight. As the arms are pushing out focus on the
back, chest, lats and abdominal muscles and also on keeping your
palms and thumbs as tight as possible.

This remarkable technique is not only one of blocking, hitting or pushing, but rather a unique method of trapping an opponents single or a one two punch, or even a leg attack and also a arm and leg combination. This will be shown in detail in the sixth and final chapter.

The Closing

In the last action of tora guchi push in right forward sanchin dachi, with a semi-circular action bring up the right hand upto the left then bring both hands together with a small circular action with the right hand resting on top of the left in line with the 'tanden' or lower abdomen. At the same time bring the right foot back to the left in musubi dachi, turning the hand inwards to return to the 'yoi' position. As the hands turn in wards inhale once then exhale in small bursts of air (about five to six times) until all the air is expelled pushing out and keeping the abdomen tensed with each exhaled burst.

This action will keep the abdomin and low back muscles contracted till the end of the kata. After a three second hold at the 'yoi' position bring the hands at the sides for another three seconds, and at this point relax the tension and then 'Rei' (bow).

The Sanchin Relaxation

With the tremendous isometric and isotonic tension created during the performance of Sanchin kata, and more so if the kata is done repeatedly three or more times, it not only is important but mandatory to relax the body immediately after.

Stand in hachiji dachi with the arms outstretched in line with the shoulders palms facing the ground. Now simply breathe deeply but without any strain in and out for about a minute. This position will automatically enable *thoracic respiration* and help in relaxing the entire body especially the rib-cage and abdominal musculature. The 'scapula' or shoulder blades return to their normal position enabling the rib cage to expand and retract to their maximum capacity which also relaxes the abdominal muscles and enhances the heart rate to near normal. Notice that as the breath is inhaled the outstretched arms will rise and on exhalation will be lowered thus relaxing the deltoid, bicep and tricep muscles and with the relaxed open palm both the forearm muscles the 'extensors and flexors loose their tension. Standing in hachiji stance (wide leg stance) ensures that the weight of the body is evenly distributed on both legs loosening up the tension from the lower back to the gluteals, quadriceps, hamstring as well as the inner and outer thigh muscles. There will be a slight strain on the calf muscles but these muscles can easily be relaxed by sitting down with one leg outstretched and the other tucked in and thereafter by pulling on the foot towards you and holding this position for 30 sec to one minute, and repeating the same with the other foot.

Chapter V

SHIME: Correcting the Sanchin Kata

1. Introduction

"SHIME", is how an Instructor or Sensei trains his or her students in Sanchin kata in progressing from a beginner to advanced level. This type of training is a one-on-one between the student and his or her Sensei and should be in keeping with the training level as well as the physical condition of the student being trained. The more senior the student, the harder the training, but if the student's physical condition is weak (after a sickness, or a long absence) then the Sensei would go easier on the severity of Sanchin shime training.

When training in other katas, the Sensei will point out the incorrect stances, blocking, punching or kicking actions, timing and other inconstancies that we all are prone to do. Sometimes the sensei will attack at the time of a block to see if that block is being performed correctly.

However during Sanchin and Tensho the correction is continuous for the entire duration of the kata done through physical contact by the Sensei to the student, and sometimes by two or more Instructors on one student at the same time. In fact this happened to all the Chief Instructors who were present at the 1982

Gasshuku in Okinawa, and Sanchin "Shime" was performed on us by Sensei Higa, Sensei Kina, Sensei An'Ichi Miyagi, and Sensei Morio Higaonna. That is one Sanchin shime I will never forget.

Many Instructors of other Goju and Karate Styles are of the opinion that the slapping or hitting aspect by the Sensei on the student, is merely for show, and is not relevant to the training of Sanchin kata.

This could not be further from the truth. The name itself - "SANCHIN" - refutes this. Sanchin refers to *Three Battles* that of the body, mind and spirit and the ultimate integration of all three into ONE composite, unified element. This part of sanchin shime is as essential as correcting the stance, or aligning the spine and shoulders of the student. The slapping of the shoulders, and thighs admittedly hurts, but should not in any way hamper the performance of the kata, and the practitioner should be in a state of "NO MIND", just as in meditation. The intention of the Sensei is not to randomly keep hitting the student, but rather to teach the student to keep his mind on the performance and not on the slaps or hits he is taking.

The following points should be kept in mind during *SHIME* training:

2. The Feet Positions

As the practitioner begins the Sanchin kata, the Sensei will first test the Sanchin dachi or stance, by seeing that the stance is correct and then by putting his fingers under the arch of the feet to access that the sole of the feet and the toes are firmly gripping the floor.

3. The toe grip

Step behind the student, and lift the small toe on either or both feet. If the gripping action is incorrect, the little toes will easily lift off. Remember, that if the little toe lifts off, it means that the Achilles tendon is relaxed making the Sanchin dachi weak.

4. The legs knees and thighs

For the next two steps, he may step back to see that in moving the student does not sway to the sides. He will also notice that the pelvis moves with the stepping action, and not separately. The Sensei will then test the tension in the Achilles

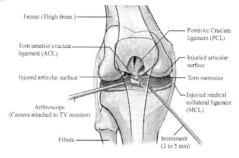

Knee Joint

tendon, the calf muscles, the back of the knees, the front and back of the thighs and the inner and outer thigh.

An important point of note here. A lot of Karatekas complain of pain in the knee joints, and one of the possible causes could be an incorrect Sanchin stance. The feet must not be turned too far inwards, because the tension and the torque strength put in the thighs, twists the knee joint putting unnecessary strain on the *"collateral ligaments"* as well as the knee cap or *"patella"*. If not corrected, over time, this could weaken the knee joint making it a potential risk for a dislocation. Always note that the center of the knee must be directly over and in line with the second toe. This positioning keeps the tension on the thigh muscles and not on the knee joint, as does an incorrect Sanchin stance.

Starting from below, the ankle joint should be in alignment with the foot and both the calf muscles should be tensed. Gentle to medium pressure should be applied on the outer and inner areas of the knee joint to see that these joints are stable. The testing of the outer thigh muscles is done by touching them and slapping them at mid-center.

5. Buttocks, Core & Anal lock

Now working upwards, the buttocks and the pelvis are the next in line to be corrected. The buttocks should be tensed and strong especially at the confluence of the buttocks and the hamstrings. If they are not tensed they should be hit with an open palm to alert the student to keep them tensed. The anus should also be tensed and locked throughout the performance.

6. The Inner Thighs

The inner thighs are tested by a gedan geri lightly or hard depending on the level of the student.

7. The Abdominals - Core muscles

The pelvic girdle is the most important area, and special attention by the Sensei should be noticed here. The pelvis should be tilted backward (see figure: the lumbar curve extreme left) though when explaining to the students, its easier for them to understand if you say "tilt your hips forward". The abdominal muscles including the obliques should be uniform in tension from the pubic upto the solar plexus. There should be no movement of the abdomen during inhalation and exhalation. except for muscular contraction during kime. The abdomen may be felt, punched or slapped to feel the uniform pressure and contraction.

When the pelvis is tilted "forwards" (in actuality backwards), the lumbar spine straightens out, which decreases the natural curvature of the back and tightens the lower abdominal muscles, which include the obliques, the transverse abdominals, and the rectus abdominals. The discs shorten their spaces and the spine becomes compressed.

This makes the body heavy, and rooted to the ground. The sanchin stance is not meant for fast movement, but to stand your ground, as the body naturally becomes strong at the core, and heavy on the soles of the feet.

On the other side of the fence, when the pelvis moves forward (See figure: The lumbar back: extreme right) or in other words when the hips are pushed backward, and the butt sticks out, the lumbar spine curves inward, increasing pressure on L4-L5-S1 vertebra.

At this point the Sensei may put his forearm on the small of the back of the student and if there is a gap at the lumbar curvature push the fingers of his other hand through the gap, informing the student to straighten up at this area.

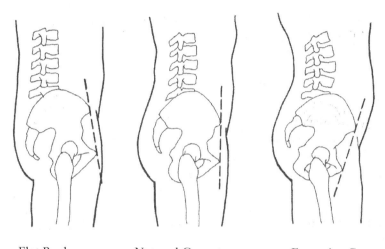

Flat Back   Natural Curvature   Excessive Curvature

The Sensei should now feel the upper, mid and lower abdomen and see that the tension is equally strong at all three areas, and at the solar plexus. This is done by feeling, palpitating the rectus abdominals, and by hitting with open palm, depending on the level and condition of the student.

8. Oblique Muscle Contraction

Moving behind the student, the Sensei should place his thumbs just over the kidney area, and notice the tension of the oblique muscles, and that tension should remain the same during inhalation and exhalation, throughout the performance of the kata. To practice this the Sensei should ask the student to remove his uwagi and to tie his obi (belt) as tightly as possible while breathing out and pulling his stomach inwards. Now he should request the student to perform the kata. As the student begins, the Sensei should put two fingers of each hand inside the obi at the kidney area, with a constant upward pressure as if trying to lift his fingers out. If the tension is correct the fingers will not come out, but if the tension of the oblique muscle is intermittent and incorrect the fingers will easily slip out.

9. Abdominal Suction

At a very senior level an advanced technique is what I have termed as the "Abdominal Suction". This unique way of testing the power of the abdominal or core muscle group, is to take a 6"-8" diameter, glass mixing bowl, covering the abdominal area just below the rib cage and below the navel. Now push the stomach into the bowl bending over at the waist, breathe out and pull in the stomach as strongly as you can, making sure that there is no gap between the bowl and the stomach. If done correctly it will create a strong vacuum, and the bowl will be held by the vacuum created by all the abdominal muscles. Keep your hands just in front of the bowl, and learn to move in sanchin dachi forward and back. On mastering this, try performing the kata with the bowl attached to the stomach wall. Do this technique only with a teacher or partner present, as the glass bowl may fall and shatter. The main aim here is to see that there is no movement of the abdominal wall, and if there is any relaxation or in and out movement of the abs, the bowl will immediately fall.

10. Punching & Kamae

Moving in front of the student, the Sensei should notice that the punching and kamae actions are done correctly and in sync to the breathing. During the action of pulling the punching arm inwards as well as the punching action itself, the forearm should be in contact with the body.

11. Resistance on Blocking and Punching actions

The Sensei can test this by giving slight to heavy resistance during the pulling and punching action. Also at the end of the punch during kime a slight push or pull on the fist will ascertain if this action is correct or not. As one hand is doing the punching action, the Sensei must also test the other hand (in yoko uke) by giving resistance at the fist level, upwards, downwards, to the right and to the left. To test the overall stability, the Sensei can also give resistance from back to the pulling action of the hand just prior to the punching action. If the balance is strong the student will not move, but if the balance and stance is incorrect the student will falter and lose his stance and concentration.

12. The Shoulders

Moving behind again, feel the tension on the latissimus dorsi or lat muscles, as well as the chest muscles (*pectoralis minor and major*) and that there is no relaxation during the entire Sanchin kata. Also note that the neck is pulled inwards, and that the neck muscles are tensed.

13. Striking the Shoulders

The Sensei should place his open palms on either shoulders and just below the trapezius muscles, and strike this area slightly or hard to see if the concentration of the student remains focused on the kata. Depending on the force of the slap on this area, even light blows are painful and sting a lot. If the practitioner is not focused on the kata, he will loose concentration and may even stop mid way in the performance. Hence it is important that the Sensei inform the student that he is going to slap, this area, by putting pressure just prior to the kime, at the end of the punching or double hand actions. A word of caution. The area slapped is just over and above the *scapularis* or shoulder blade, where the skin is thinnest. The slapping at this area normally results in deep discoloration and even bruising. If excessive and painful, ice application, and a cold cream will do wonders in healing it faster. This bruising normally lasts a day or three at the most.

During nukite tsugi, pressure should be given on the palms upwards, downwards, inwards and outwards, to see the tension is constant.

As the student commences the tora guchi action, resistance on the open palms of the student must be given especially to test the smooth confluence of the inhalation and exhalation. If the student does this correctly by pushing the breath into the abdominal area, he will easily be able to counter the resistance and push his hands forwards. If not, he will invariably loose his concentration and his balance as well.

14. The Neck

As mentioned earlier, the neck should be retracted with the chin, just over the sternum. The eyes should be focused as if looking at the horizon in the distance, straight ahead. This position of the neck will enable strong inhalation and exhalation, with the Adam's Apple retracted and keep all the neck muscles contracted to assist strongly in respiration. The *sterno mastoid* muscles on either side of the neck are amongst the strongest muscles of the body. And these should remain in contraction throughout the performance of the kata.

With both hands grasp the neck and gently squeeze the neck increasing the pressure depending on the level of the student. This test should be performed on advanced students and not on beginners or even intermediates. If the student gives any indication of gasping, coughing, stop immediately. If the neck is positioned correctly and the neck muscles properly tensed, he will be able to breath in and out without any discomfort.

15. The solar plexus lock

This action is rather difficult to explain, and should be seen and then taught and subsequently practised. First, in a standing position in Sanchin dachi, relax the abdominal area completely. A partner should place his thumb or finger exactly on the solar plexus, with very slight pressure. Now tense the abdominal muscles. Even with the abdominals tensed, the solar plexus will be relatively soft and open to attack. Concentrating on this area lift the entire abdominal wall up and towards the solar plexus. If done correctly, the topmost striation of the abdominal rectus will overlap the solar plexus and cover it, thus protecting this vital point. Before any form of hitting the solar plexus is attempted, the Sensei must ensure that the student has indeed locked the abdominal wall by feeling with the thumb or finger. Only when he is sure that the practitioner has locked this vital point, should he attempt a nukite strike. If the abdominal wall has locked in place correctly, the nukite strike or even a seiken tsugi will literally bounce off without any discomfort to the student.

Chapter VI

Improving Sanchin performance

1. Introduction

Aside from Sanchin and Tensho Katas, traditional Goju Ryu, is also unique in the development of *"Hojo Undo"* or supplementary exercises, to develop hard and soft power. This involves partner training, and the use of specialized training implements. With the exception of the *"Kongo-Ken"* an elongated "U" shaped iron instrument closed at both ends, which originated in Hawaii, all other training implements come from Okinawa.

kongo ken

Other training implements are the *"makiwara"* or punching post, *"nigri game"* or heavy Jars used by gripping the neck of the jars for increasing gripping strength, *"ishi-sashi"* or stone kettle-bells for strengthening the whole body, *"chishi"* or a wooden handle heavy at one end for the development of upper body strength, and *"tan"* or barbell.

Partner training consists of *"kakei kaketae"* or pushing hands and is one exercise that really develops the *deltoids* or shoulder muscles. It also develops and aids in learning various techniques to off balance one's opponent crucial in self defense and sparring.

Partner training is essential in learning and training in Sanchin Kata. Another training method is *"ude-te"* or arm conditioning. This is performed when partners collide their arms on the inside and outside edge of the bone (ulna & radial bones). Over time these bones get stronger and become devastating weapons of defense. If an untrained attacker attacks a karateka who had undergone this training, with just a blocking action he has the power and technique to easily fracture the attacking limb.

When training with traditional implements make sure that your physical condition is on par with the training implement. For example chi shi's, nigri game jars, and ishi shashi come in different sizes and or weightages, so pick the right weight in line with your current physical condition. Beginners should always start with a light weight and slowly go onto the heavier weights as they progress. Training methodologies like pull ups, push ups, free squats, *kakei kaketae,* and other free hand exercises will give you strength, but training with the traditional implements will give you a whole lot of power as well. Always check the equipment you are going to practise with, and when practising make sure that you have enough space around you.

Now we come to a very interesting "Oxymoron" *(a figure of speech in which apparently contradictory terms appear in conjunction),* namely "GOJU", or Hard & Soft. Though we all understand this in relation to the style, how does it explain a hard punch from a soft one? Or does a soft technique actually exist, and if so what type of damage does it do? And finally how does one do it.

On researching through the internet, I found the following explanation, but not necessarily the correct one:

"In keeping with the hard and soft meaning of Goju, so the strike with an open hand are termed 'soft' and strikes with a closed fist or elbow are

termed 'hard'. Often the 'hard' strikes are to the soft areas of the body, and 'soft' strikes are to the hard areas".

I personally am of the opinion that it is not the type of technique that differentiates a 'hard' strike from a 'soft' strike but rather it's the execution of the strike that makes it 'hard' or 'soft'.

Shihan Higaonna has often explained the difference between a hard technique and a soft technique, by equating the former of hitting an object with a hard stick, and the latter by hitting an object with a wet towel.

In 2003 I had taken a team to Okinawa, and for the first three days our sessions were taken by Shihan Higaonna. It was during one of these sessions where I actually saw a demonstration of the awesome power of a "soft" technique. Shihan was explaining the four sided turning technique from Kata Sisochin using "*jodan shotei zuki and a gedan shotei barai*" simultaneously. To demonstrate this technique he asked one of our senior students "Juggie" to do a strong and fast chudan geri at him. The first three kicks were slow, and after being told to do the technique as hard and as fast as he could, he finally let loose a powerful mid level front kick at Shihan.

The next instant, and what seemed like a lazy deflection and push had seen Juggie literally lift off the floor and flying a good seven feet away to land flat on his back, and without any recollection of what had just taken place. When I examined him, there was no bruising on the chest where the shotei tsugi had been targeted. If that had been a hard contact I am positive that the ribs would have been fractured. So I can only surmise that it was in fact a "soft" technique.

To achieve this type of power take years of Karate training and a lot of Sanchin training as well.

At one of our International Gasshaku's, all Senior Chief Instructors were being trained in the use of "*chi-shi*" & "*nigri game*" by the late Sensei An'Ichi Miyagi alongwith Sensei Aragaki, and we were informed that without Hojo Undo training regularly, we would never understand the ''JU' aspects of Sanchin and Tensho training.

2. Chi-shi Training for Sanchin Kata

Following are one of the exercises with the Chi Shi specific for Sanchin Training:

Fig. 1. Hold chi-shi
in a pronated grip.

Fig.2. Lift chi-shi
with the same grip.

Fig.3. Twist the wrist to
hold Chi-shi upright.

Fig.4. Pull back arm as in
preparation for a punch.

Fig.5. Straighten arm to full extension.

Fig. 6. With control bend elbow to yoko uke position.

Fig. 7. Straighten arm again to full extension.

Fig. 8. Return to original position. Do 10 reps & repeat with other arm.

3. Kettlebell Training for Power & Strength

Though the origin of the Kettlebell began well in the 1800's in Russia where strong men of that time used them to increase their strength and endurance, its popularity is just increasing by leaps and bounds. In traditional hojo undo a similar type of implement is also used, and is called "ishi sashi".

One particular and the main stay of any kettlebell training program is the kettlebell swing, and is one of the most effective exercise to gain massive strength and muscular endurance. It's a total body exercises, using the momentum of the swing for power rather than lifting the kettlebell. Below is the technique used in this great exercise.

Fig 1. Stand in front of the kettlebell at about arms distance, with feet slightly wider than the shoulders.

Fig. 2. Lower yourself into a half squat position and reach out to grip the kettlebell. Do not round the back.

Fig. 3. Keeping your back straight (natural state) lift the kettlebell and let it swing between your legs.

Fig. 4. Now straighten up, swinging the kettlebell up and in line with your shoulders. Remember to exhale on the upswing.

Fig.5. At the apex of your swing, lower the kettlebell back between your knees and repeat for the required number of reps, then rest the kettlebell on the out swing.

Note: Repeat this for 75 swings with a 24Kg kettlebell. For beginners, I suggest a 12 to 15 Kg kettlebell for 3 sets of 15 to 20 reps each.

4. Core Training

In Chapter1, I had briefly mentioned the 'core' in relation to Sanchin posture in general. Most of us know that the 'core' refers to the abdominal and pelvic muscles, and most of us would be wrong. In actual fact the core muscles involved extend from the shoulders to the knees, and core exercises may be quite a revelation. Abdominal crunches, sit ups are just not enough. In fact the abdominal muscles or a six-pack is just a very small part of the core. When sports Therapists and Physiotherapists refer to the core group of muscles they are talking about many different muscles that stabilize the spine and pelvis, and run the entire length of the trunk. When these muscles contract they stabilize the spine, pelvis and shoulder girdle and create a solid base of support, which is exactly what happens in the correct Sanchin posture. It is precisely because of this strong stability, that in Sanchin kata we are able to generate tremendous power from the upper and lower limbs.

On a general note, the core muscles also make it possible to stand upright and to move on our two feet. They also control movements, transfer energy, shift body weight and enable us to make sudden changes in any direction. A strong core distributes the stresses of weight-bearing and supports the back. Hence any core-conditioning exercise program has to target all these muscles to be effective.

Core Muscle Group:

The following list includes the most commonly known core muscles and also the lesser known ones:

- *Rectus Abdominis - Probably the most well known of all muscle groups also called the 'six-pack' and is located along the front of the abdomen.*
- *Erector Spinae - This group of three muscles runs from the neck down to the lower back on both sides of the spine.*
- *Multifidus - located under the 'Erector Spinae' alongside the vertebral column, and they extend and rotate the spine.*
- *External Obliques - located on the side and front of the abdomen.*
- *Internal Obliques - located under the External Obliques, running in the opposite direction.*
- *Transverse Abdominis (TVA) - located under the obliques and the deepest of all the abdominal muscles. It is also called the 'corset' of the human body as it completely encases the spine and waist for protection and stability.*
- *Hip Flexors - located in the front of the pelvis in line with the pubic bone and the upper thigh. They include: 'psoas major', illiacus, rectus femoris, pectineus, and sartorius,*
- *Gluteus medius and minimus - located at the side of the hip.*

- *Gluteus maximus, hamstring group, & piriformis - located in the rear of the hip and upper thigh.*
- *Hip Adductors - located at medial thigh.*

Importance of Strong Core Strength

If the back muscles are not as strong as the abdominal muscles, it will eventually lead to low back pain and could also lead to spondylosis and sciatica. Weak core muscles will also lead to a loss of the correct lumbar curve and a swayback posture. A strong core will help maintain the proper posture and reduce strain on the spine.

Strong Core is Mandatory for Athletic Excellence

If you have ever seen a Olympic gymnast perform his routine on the Roman Rings, it will immediately bring to mind the superb strength and control which is only possible with a highly developed core. And this holds good for all athletic endeavors. Because the muscles of the trunk and torso stabilize the spine from the pelvis to the neck and shoulder, they allow the transfer of power to the arms and legs. All powerful movements originate from the center of the body out, and never from the limbs alone. Before any strong rapid muscle contractions can occur in the extremities, the spine must be solid and stable and the greater the stability in the core muscles the more powerful the extremities can contract.

Training the core muscles helps correct postural imbalances that could lead to injuries. The most important benefit is to develop functional fitness; the type of fitness that can allow a person to do rock climbing, sky diving, or any endeavor you may want to without fear of injury.

5. Core Training Exercises

Core strengthening exercises are most effective when the torso works as a solid unit when both anterior and posterior muscles contract simultaneously, multi joint movements are performed and stabilization of the spine is monitored. Abdominal bracing is a basic technique and used during core exercise training. In fact during kata training at the "YOI" position this abdominal bracing should be performed. To correctly brace, you should gently pull your navel back in toward your spine. This action primarily contracts your 'transverse abdominus', or the natural 'corset' of the body. Furthermore, keep breathing evenly and never hold your breath.

Exercises that work the core are most effective when they engage many muscles throughout the torso that cross several joints and work in concert to engage stability. The following is a simple but effective core workout and it doesn't take much time or equipment but covers all the core muscles:

V Leg Hold Outs
This is an powerful and excellent exercise to train the core muscles. Work first on getting the legs off the floor with just the head and shoulder lift, and hold for upto a minute. Only then try to raise the upper body also off the floor and hold position for upto 20 seconds.

Plank Exercise
Lie down on your front with your forearms perpendicular to your shoulders. Now, raise your hips, so that you are

supporting yourself on your forearms and on the balls of your feet only. Start with holding this position for 30 seconds and work gradually for two minutes. Once you have achieved this you can try the advanced version. Hold the basic position for a minute, then keeping your balance and your hips properly aligned, raise your right hand and hold for 15 seconds. Then return to basic position and immediately raise your left hand. Return to the basic position, then raise your left leg and hold for 15 seconds.

Return to the basic position and now raise your right hand and left leg for 15 seconds. Back to basic position and now raise your left hand and right leg for 15 seconds. Now return to basic position and hold for the last 30 seconds. Rest. At any point if you feel strain on the low back stop immediately. This obviously means that your core is still not strong enough, or that you are not holding the Plank position correctly.

Straight Leg Hold Outs

This is an excellent core workout exercise and especially for strengthening the low back area. Note that it is very important from the beginning position to keep the lower back in constant contact with the floor. If at any time during the performance of this exercise, you find your lower back coming off the floor stay in the last previous position where your back was on the floor and hold at this level. As your core gets stronger you will be able to hold till the final positions with feet just one inch off the floor.

Also the arms may remain alongside the body, and not clasped above the chest, which I have shown so the the lower back floor contact may be seen.

Push ups:

Lie on your front, with palms or with fists of the first two knuckles, on the floor a bit wider than your shoulders and with the chest directly over your hands.

Rest only on your palms(or knuckles) and on the balls of your feet. From the back of your head to your heels the body should be in as straight a line as possible, throughout the complete range of motion of the push up. Take 4 seconds to lower yourself, until your chest just touches the floor and then push yourself up taking 3 to 4 seconds.

Squats

Stand with feet just slightly more than shoulder width. Keeping the natural curve in your spine, commence the lowering of your body from the hips by imagining that you are sitting on a stool behind you. Stop the movement when your lower thighs are parallel to the ground and keep your knees behind your toe-line. Return to start position, and do a small pelvic tilt and release it before doing your next squat. Breathe in on the way down, and hold in the squat position, then release the breath as you come up.

6. Yogic posture & Breathing techniques

(To enhance breathing strength, flexibility and core development).

Yoga postures or '*Asanas*' and breathing techniques or '*Pranayama*', will undoubtedly help, in strengthening one's performance of not only Sanchin and Tensho but all kata's in our system. This is because the dynamic postures involve the whole body, while the breathing techniques enhance and improve the vital capacity of the lungs. Certain special postures can also teach us the apparent difference of using our muscles in the normal contracted position (hard) but also in the non-contracted position (soft). For example, a strong contracted abdomen may withstand a really all out punch, but this can also be accomplished by keeping the outer muscle wall (*rectus abdominus*) relaxed but with the deep inner muscle wall (*transverse abdominus*) tensed, and once mastered is much easier than keeping the entire abdominus muscle tensed. This is what takes time and constant training. Yoga techniques can help us achieve this level of expertise.

Furthermore, Sanchin kata is a highly rigorous exercise, and doing even 5 repetitions can leave one exhausted, and a prime candidate for DOMS (Delayed Onset Muscular Soreness) or the pain and stiffness that sets in hours or even a day after. This state could be avoided by performing the "Surya Namaskar" (a Yogic exercise) which can be done as a warm up and as a cool down prior and post to doing Sanchin kata. It literally means salutation to the sun, and is in fact made up of twelve different asanas or poses, performed in a particular sequence, with the correct breathing. At a deeper and advanced level it is also used in *"Chakra Meditation'*, or meditating on the 7 centers of the body. A variation of this technique is used in our system and is shown in Sensei Higaonna's Book "VOL I Traditional Karatedo Okinawa Goju Ryu" under Warm up, termed as 'Push up - Cat Style'.

It is often mentioned that the power of Sanchin kata lies in the tanden or Lower stomach, and in Yoga there are several abdominal techniques that helps in training the entire abdominopelvic structure, and is used in Yoga as a cleansing exercise to normalize the '*fire*' of digestion.

Before proceeding into the performance, a word of caution. Women should not do this technique during their menstrual cycles. Persons having High Blood Pressure, Ulcers or any type of Hernia, should avoid doing 'Agni Sara', '*Uddiyana Bandha*' & '*Nauli*'.

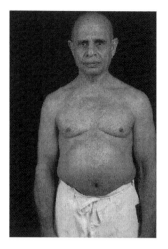
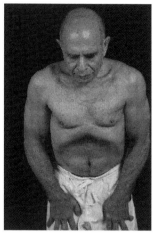

AGNI SARA

Performance:

1). Stand with feet about 12" apart.

2). Lean your body over between 45 and 55 degrees forward resting your palms on your thighs just above the knees.

3). Keep the knees slightly flexed with the head down and relaxed along with the abdominal and back muscles.

4). Breathe in allowing the abdomen to expand naturally.

5). In 'agni sara', each part of the abdomen has to be consciously pulled in one at a time. Now, breathe out and focus on the area just above the pubis, pulling it inwards.

6). Continue exhaling and now pull in the stomach at the mid or belly button level.

7). Continue exhaling and now focus on pulling in the area of the upper stomach solar plexus level inwards ending with the intercostal muscles of your rib cage.

8). The exhalation should press the abdomen and chest inwards while at the same time you should feel the rounded back being pushed upwards.

9). Immediately at the end of your exhalation, commence inhaling allowing the abdominal muscles to relax in reverse order. First the intercostal muscles of the chest and upper abdomen, then mid abdomen and lastly the muscles just above the pubis.

10). Start out with 20 repetitions and slowly work your way up to 100 to 150 reps, which should take about 3 to 4 months of daily practice.

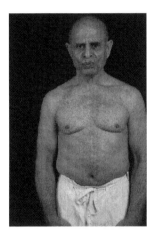 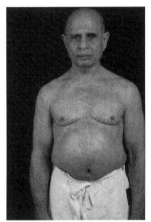 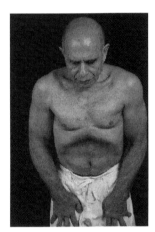

These practices should be performed preferably in the morning on an empty stomach, after evacuation of the bowels. Done correctly the stomach should form a wave-like action.

The *'agni sara'* yoga technique should be learnt first before trying the following two techniques called *'uddiyana bandha'* & *'nauli'.*

UDDIYANA BANDHA

In Sanchin kata performance at the point of each *"kime"* or focus, where for a second, the entire body is tensed to the maximum, there are certain areas where a locking mechanism should take place. Specifically the anus, solar plexus, and the glottis. As the breath is exhaled maximally at the end of the punching actions, the double uke, the nukite tsugi, and the tora guchi actions, the lower abdomen is lifted upwards, contracting the sphincter muscles, while the rectus abdominal muscles are pushed up covering or locking the solar plexus. At the same time, the neck should be retracted, and the glottis locked so that the neck muscles are fully tensed protecting the vulnerable throat and Adam's apple.

The practice of "uddiyana bandha" has helped me quite a bit in understanding and performing the three locks as mentioned above.

By definition, "uddiyana bandha" comes under the section of pranayama or breathing exercises. However it is also a method to help one understand and perform the three energy locks in Yoga. Though all three locks are applied in this particular technique, it is the abdominal lock that is mainly predominant. Its function is to control the flow of energy and breath in the body.

Performance of "uddiyana bandha":

2. Begin is the same position as in 'agni sara'.

3. Inhale to your fullest amount then exhale maximally.

4. Now hold your breath, and do a fake inhalation, or in other words do the action of inhaling without actually pulling any air into the body. This action should act like a vacuum, pulling the entire abdomen in and up into the cavity now formed, under the rib cage.

5. Hold this position for a second or two. As you progress over time, hold this position for upto 5 seconds. Repeat this cycle 5 to 7 times.

6. Now release the vacuum position, by relaxing the abdomen and inhaling slowly and easily.

'Uddiyana bandha' can be quite strenuous and energizing. It tones, cleans and massages the organs of the digestive system, leading to heal and normalize the digestive process. In fact this practice stretches the respiratory diaphragm, and with practice it will lengthen the diaphragm's muscle and connective tissue fibers keeping the chest wall and diaphragm in an optimum state of health. In Sanchin kata performance at the point of each "*kime*" or focus, where for a second, the entire body is tensed to the maximum, there are certain areas where a locking mechanism should take place. Specifically the anus, solar plexus, and the glottis.

NAULI

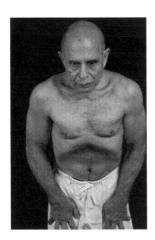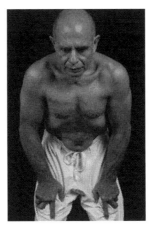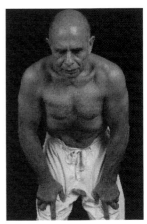

The main benefit of this particular exercise for Sanchin practioners, is that it gives one total control of the entire abdominal structure in general, and in particular the rectus abdominus.

'Nauli' is essentially a cleansing exercise and comes under this heading in Hatta Yoga. It cleans the internal organs of the digestive system and tones the abdominal region by a side to side rolling motion of the central, left and right rectus abdominal muscle.

This is a highly advanced technique and quite difficult to perform and best learned from a qualified Yoga teacher, which I most definitely recommend. As the pressure in the chest and abdominal cavity is seriously increased, it could cause discomfort and even pain. It is also contraindicated for pregnant women, or persons with hernias, hypertension, heart diseases, ulcers, and various stomach ailments.

"NAULI" in Sanskrit translates to mean *"churning"* in English. It is also one of the six main purification techniques recommended in the "Hata Yoga Pradipika". A commentary on Nauli by Swami Mukitibodhananda states that *"when the different systems of the body have been purified, the overall result is that energy can flow freely through the body.*

Chapter Vll

Sanchin fighting techniques

1. Introduction

Sanchin Kata is essentially a breathing kata, and for developing both 'hard' and 'soft' power. However in a close quarter situation, its techniques can be used with relative ease and devastating force.

2. Leg Attacks

Foot trap

Fig. 1. Attack chu dan tsugi

Fig 2. Chu dan uke block and trap opponents foot.

Fig 3. Trapping foot counter
with jo dan tsugi at throat.

Fig 4. Close up of foot trapping

Inward knee Lock

Fig 1. Attack with chu dan tsugi
and block with inside chudan uke.

Fig 2. Slide in and block and
press down on opponents
shin with you leg.

Fig Finish with jodan tsugi
at opponents throat.

Fig 4 Close up of inside knee lock.

Rear Knee Drop

Fig 1. Attack with chu dan tsugi
& block with chudan uke.

Fig 2. Quickly turn outwards,
placing your left leg behind
opponents knee.

Fig 3. Trap opponents arm as in a
straight arm bar and commence
pressing your opponents leg with
your left knee behind his right leg.

Fig 4. Continue putting pressure
on arm and leg of opponent.

Fig 5. Hit the back of the
head with ridge hand strick
with pressure on the knee.

Fig 6 Giving pressure on his
leg bring him on his knee
and punch or grab the vital
center at the back of neck.

3. Open Hand Locks and Attacks

Fig 1. Opponent attacks
with ge-dan tsugi.

Fig 2. Attacker commences
Left ge dan tsugi attack.

Elbow smash and knee kick

Fig 3. Block with open
hand ge-dan barai.

Fig 4. Grab attackers left hand with
your right hand and apply a left
mawashi hiji-ate to attackers neck.

Fig 5. Instantly grab opponents
back of head and pull him down.

Fig 6. As you pull him down apply
a hiza geri to his rib cage.

Open hand block with nukite strike.

Fig 1. Opponent commences attack.

Fig 2. Opponent attacks
with right gedan tsugi.

Fig 3. Defender blocks with
left open hand gedan barai.

Fig 4. Immediately counter
with right Nukite strike
at opponents throat.

Double open hand block and leg lock.

Fig 1. Attacker in ready position.

Fig 2. Attacker launches
a mai-geri attack.

Fig3. Using tsuri ashi move quickly to your right, trapping opponents leg in a kosa uke.

Fig 4. Twisting your arms in a clockwise direction pull the attackers leg towards you.

Fig 5. Twist your opponent by applying pressure on the knee.

Fig 6. Commence a left ge-dan geri.

Fig 7. Complete the technique by applying a gedan geri at opponent's groin.

Conclusion

In conclusion I would like to repeat once more as I have in the beginning of this book, that to truly understand Sanchin kata you have to practice it daily, reading about it will enhance your understanding, but you will never comprehend it unless you actually practice it daily.

Sensei Higaonna has advised that this kata be practiced 5 times every day, preferably in the morning. It can also be practiced in the evening, but I would not advise practicing it in the night before sleeping. With the adrelin and immense blood flow flushing the system it would be practically impossible to sleep. As with any other exercise endeavor, practice on an empty stomach.

Practicing this kata in the dojo is fine, but practicing it on a sea shore, a mountain top, or even under a waterfall brings about a far greater sense of appreciation of ourselves and our natural surroundings.

We all live on this tiny planet we call Earth and it amazes me that each and everyone of us has the potential to make this a heaven or totally destroy it and ourselves in annihilation. Practicing Sanchin every day has made me more calmer, more patient, and given me a greater understanding of myself and others around me.

I sincerely hope that this book helps all practioners of Sanchin kata to understand the science and appreciate its many attributes and benifits. I also hope that others take up serious research on this amazing and fascinating form.

With daily practice, your body will keep getting stronger, your mind will be far less cluttered, and your spirit indomitable. In short "SANCHIN" - Three Battles.

Terminology

(Japanese to English terminology used in this book)

Japanese	English
Japanese	**English**
jodan	Upper area (throat to head)
chudan	middle area (solar plexus to throat)
Gedan	lower area (below solar plexus)
kamae	combative posture
hajime	begin
yame	stop
kime	focus
rei	bow
yoi	ready
hidari	left
migi	right
dachi	stance
shiko dachi	straddle leg stance
sanchin dachi	hourglass stance
Zenkutsu dachi	front stance
musubi dachi	formal attention stance (heels together feet at an angle)
tsugi (zuki)	punch
seiken tsugi	fore fist punch
yama tsugi	mountain punch
kizami tsugi	leading punch (jab)
nukite tsugi	finger thrust (spear hand strike)
keri (geri)	kick

mae geri (keage)	front snap kick
mae geri (kekomi)	front thrust kick
mawashi geri	round house kick
ushiro geri	back thrust kick
yoko geri (keage)	side snap kick
yoko geri (kekomi)	side thrust kick
kansetsu geri	stamping kick, joint kick
hiza geri	knee kick
uke	block
age uke (jodan)	rising block
chudan uke	inside circular block
gedan barai	downward block
josokutai	ball of foot
sokuto	edge of foot
kakato	heel of foot
haisoku	instep
mawashi uke (toraguchi)	circular block
tora guchi	tiger's mouth

Appendix I

SANCHIN PARAMETERS OF AMA INDIA STUDENTS

The following are pre and post Sanchin Kata parameters taken of my students. These are my findings. However, far more research has to be done to reach a definitive conclusion on the many benifits of Sanchin Kata.

No. 1. Male 31 yrs. San Dan. Height: 5'.9". Weight: 70Kg. Smoker. Exercise pre Sanchin: 1 hour.

PRE SANCHIN: Pulse: 123min. O2.: 99%. BP: 160/90 mmHg. Time of Kata: 2:20:35.

POST SANCHIN: Pulse: 116min. O2.99% BP: 150/80 mmHg.

No.2. Male 50 yrs. San Dan. Height: 6'.00. Weight: 75Kg. Non Smoker. Exercise. pre Sanchin: 30 min.

PRE SANCHIN: Pulse: 92/min. O2.: 99%. BP: 150/90 mmHg.

POST SANCHIN: Sanchin time: 1:56:12. Pulse: 110/min. O2.: 98. BP: 155/105 mmHg.

No.3. Female 44 yrs. Go DanHeight:5'.0. Weight: 62 Kg. Non Smoker. Exercise pre Sanchin 90 min.

PRE SANCHIN: Pulse:71/min O2:: 99. BP: 140/80mmHg.

POST SANCHIN: Sanchin time:2:55:69 Pulse:68. O2: 99. BP: 135/80mmHg.

No.4. Male 29 yrs. San Dan. Height 5'.9.5". Weight: 62Kg. Non smoker Exercise pre Sanchin: 90 min.

PRE SANCHIN: Pulse:90/min. O2:97. BP: 110/80.mmHg

POST SANCHIN: Sanchin tme:2:05:53. Pulse:87/min. O2:98 BP:130/80 mmHg

No.5. Male. Age:36yrs. Ni Dan. Height: 6'.2". Weight: 90Kg. Exercise pre Sanchin: 20min. Non smoker.

PRE SANCHIN: Pulse:99/min. O2: 98. BP: 120/80mmHg

POST SANCHIN: Sanchin Time: 2:22:35. Pulse:92/min O2: 98. BP:130/95.

No.6. Male. Age:58 yrs. Go Dan. Height:5'.8". Weight:66Kg. Exercise pre Sanchin: 25min.

Smoker and asthma since childhood.

PRE SANCHIN: Pulse:102/min.O2: 98. BP: 160/110mmHg.

POST SANCHIN: Sanchin time:2:45:03. Pulse:115/min O2:98. BP:160/110mmHg.

No.7. Male. Age: 48 yrs. Go Dan. Height: 5'.8". Weight:81Kg. Exercise pre Sanchin:35min.

Non smoker.

PRE SANCHIN: Pulse:89/min. O2:99. BP: 140/110.mmHg.

POST SANCHIN: Sanchin time:01:47:07. Pulse:104. 02:99. BP:135/90mmHg.

No.8. Male, Age: 54 yrs. Go Dan. Height:5'.8". Weight: 81Kg. Exercise pre Sanchin:25min. Non smoker.

PRE SANCHIN: Pulse:96/min. O2.:99. BP: 150/100 mmHg.

POST SANCHIN: Sanchin time: 2:44:25. Pulse:90. O2. BP: 140/90mmHg.

9. Male. Age: 47 yrs. Yon Dan. Height: 5'.6". Weight: 72Kg. Exercise pre Sanchin:30min.

Smoker.

PRE SANCHIN: Pulse:118/min. O2:98. BP:152/100mmHg.

POST SANCHIN: Sanchin time:2:05:06. Pulse:150/min. O2:98/min. BP:130/88mmHg.

10. Male: 49 yrs. Ni Dan. Height: 5'.10". Weight:80Kg. Exercise pre Sanchin:2hrs. Non Smoker.

PRE SANCHIN: Pulse: 93/min. O2:97. BP: 130/80mmHg.

POST SANCHIN: Sanchin time:1:55:08. Pulse:127min. O2: 98. BP:140/80mmHg.

11. Male. Age: 53 yrs. Go Dan. Height:5'.8". Weight 83Kg. Exercise pre Sanchin:2hrs.

Non Smoker.

PRE SANCHIN: Pulse:110/min. O2: 97. BP:130/90 min.

POST SANCHIN: Sanchin time:2:41:24. Pulse:100/min. O2: 98. BP:140/90mmHg.

Appendix II

The Pulmonary Function Tests below were recommended by me to my students, for my own research in Sanchin Kata. I earnestly hope that many more Instructors will take the lead in researching the breathing Katas of Okinawa Goju Ryu.

Pulmonary Function Tests of AMA Students
(the names of the diagnostic centers has been
omitted for professional reasons)

PULMONARY FUNCTION TEST REPORT

NAME :	Mr. Rohimton Patel	DATE :	12-06-2012
SEX :	Male	AGE :	49 Years
REF. PHYSICIAN	Dr	SMOKER :	Yes

INTERPRETATION :

The spirogram pattern is within normal limits.
Patient has good ventilatory reserve.

DR. R.V.Chowgule
M.D., F.C.C.P.
Consultant Pulmonary Physician

Pulmonary Function Test Report

ID	450233	Date	10-04-12
Last Name	Mistry	Time	12:54:32PM
First Name	Zeenat	Temperature	23 °C
Sex	female	Rel. humidity	76 %
Age	41 Years	Ref.Doctor	R Barman
Height	156 cm	Ref.Doctor	
Weight	62 kg	Technician	Lalita
Smoker	No	Ref. From	Health Plan A+
Indication	Routine Check	Pred. Module	Udwadia etal

Spirometry

		Actual	Predicted	%Predicted
FVC	[L]	2.98	2.54	117
FEV 1	[L]	2.38	1.92	124
FEV 1 % FVC	[%]	79.75		
PEF	[L/s]	8.28	4.96	167
FEF 50	[L/s]	2.65	2.83	94
FEF 75/25	[L/s]	2.17	2.30	94
FIF 50	[L/s]	3.67		

The spirometry test is within normal limits.

DR. J.D. SUNAVALA
MD FCCP

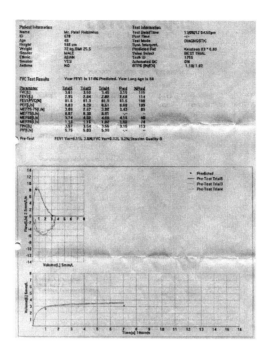

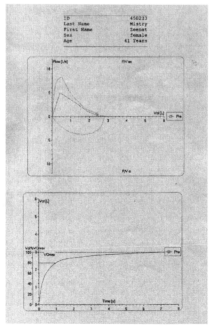

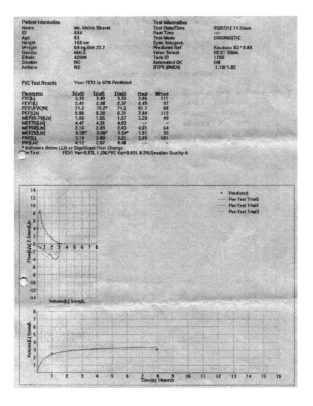

List of Illustrations

Appendix III

FAQ's on SANCHIN KATA

Questions on Sanchin Kata from my students and other Karatekas and my answers:

Q. 1. How is it that though Sanchin Kata is such an intense exercise that on performing it our pulse rate drops down. Why doesn't it increase instead?
Naveen Mahadeshwar.

A. 1. If you practice Sanchin kata without a warm up or just cold, your pulse rate will surely rise. However after a warm up and some hard training when your pulse rate is already high, and then after Sanchin your pulse rate should come down, which shows that your breathing technique is correct. Most importantly, there is very little movement, and the contraction of all the body muscles create an intense intra-abdominal pressure which coupled with the slow but forced breathing, slows down the heart. See Appendix I.

Q. 2. What are the overall health benefits of doing Sanchin, and what are the pros and cons of doing Sanchin in the evening?
Avnish Bharat Mehta.

A. 2. Regular Sanchin training will improve your strength, power, and speed. It also enhances the immune system, regulates your digestive system, calms your mind and improves your reflexes. Sanchin training in the evening is fine, but be careful when training in the night, as it may keep you wide awake, as it energizes your body making sleep difficult to come by.

Q. 3. Why should one practise Sanchin kata? Are there any side effects because of heavy and deep breathing e.g. Hernia, acidity etc.

D. B. Rai.

A. 3. If you practise Goju Ryu then you will have to practise this fundamental Kata, regardless of which style of Goju Ryu you belong to. Goju means Hard and soft, and Sanchin Kata embodies its hard aspect, which is why the Founder originated the softer breathing Kata "Tensho" to complement Sanchin. Performed correctly and under correct supervision there should be no side effects. However as with any hard training you should not practice Sanchin for upto 3 hours after a meal. Women should not practice Sanchin during their menstrual cycles, and this Kata should be avoided when recuperating from a surgery or illness.

Q. 4. Any specific time of day to practice it which will give the most benefit … foods to eat before and after…

Karl Behramfram.

A. 4. Morning is a good time, as you have rested the night before. Late afternoon is also great as your body temperature is at its warmest and evening is ok too. Don't practice at night. About 45 min before any form of training or exercise, a small carbohydrate meal will give you enough energy without tapping into your reserves. Within 30 min. after training a protein meal will go a long way in repairing and enhancing your muscles.

Q. 5. What is the practical advantage of 'SHIME' performed during the Kata.

Hitesh Parekh.

A. 5. SHIME is normally refereed to as TESTING. However I prefer to call it Correcting. It is the Sensei's duty to regularly correct the Sanchin performance of his students and this is done through shime. Please read Chapter V for a more detailed explanation.

Q. 6. Any benefits to the Renal System? *Gul Ibrahim.*

A. 6. Sanchin training benefits all systems of the body, and since it helps digestion through intense abdominal pressure, there is far greater blood circulation in the intestines leading to a healthier digestive tract.

Q.7. Benefits to the heart? Diabetes ?
Sudarshan Roongta.
A. 7. All exercise is beneficial to the heart and that goes for those with either Type 1 or Type 2 Diabetes. Regular Sanchin training will help in making the heart stronger and last longer. It may also help in controlling the Glycogen – Insulin levels for those with either type of Diabetes.

Q.8. What are the major differences between Sanchin and Tensho ?
T. Khan.
A.8. Please wait for my next book. See answer 3.

Q. 9. Are there any okuden bunkai application in Sanchin Kata ?
A. London.
A. 9. Most definitely yes there are.

Q. 10. I have heard and read that Sanchin training was extremely hard during Kanryo Higaonna's and Chogun Miyagi's times. Why don't we practise it the same way today?

B. Barucha.

A. 10. I seriously doubt if we would have any students except you perhaps? Times change and the careful Instructor changes with the times. No one that I know would continue doing Sanchin only for 3 to 4 years, before learning just one more kata.

Bibliography

Three Battles
SANCHIN
The Anatomy and Physiology of Sanchin Kata

Books:

H. David Coulter: *Anatomy of Hatha Yoga*. Motilal Banarsidas Publishers. *2004;2006;2007.*

Lee Parore: *Power Posture.* Apple Publishing Co. 2002.

Patrick Denard: *Kalaripayat*. Destiny Books. 1998; 2009.

Inge Dougans: *Complete Reflexology*. Element Books 1996

Morio Higaonna: *Traditional Karate-do - Okinawa Goju Ryu. VOL: 1* Minato Research and Publishing Co. 1985;

Morio Higaonna: *Traditional Karate-do - Okinawa Goju Ryu. VOL: 2. Minato Research and Publishing Co.1986*

Morio Higaonna: *Traditional Karate-do - Okinawa Goju Ryu. VOL: .3 Minato Research and Publishing Co.1989'*

Morio Higaonna: *Traditional Karate-do - Okinawa Goju Ryu. VOL 4. Minato Research and Publishing Co. 1990.*

History of Okinawan Goju Ryu Karate-do. Sugawara Martial Arts inc. Tokyo 1993. Brian Halpern M.D. with Laura Tucker. *The Knee Crisis Handbook.* St. Martin's press. 2003. RODALE. Life Time Media. Inc.

Dr. Michael Colgan. *Optimum Sports Nutrition. Your Competitive Edge.* Advanced Research Press.*1993.*

Philip Sandbrook MB, BS, MD, LLB, FRACP. Leslie Schrieber. MD, FRACP. Thomas Taylor. DPHIL (OXON) FRACS, FRCS (Ed). Andrew Ellis. MB BS (UNSW), FRACS(Orth), FAO Orth, A, RAAMC. *The Musculoskeletal System.* Churchill Livingstone 2001.

Mitchel Study Editor. Personal Trainer Manual - The Resource for Fitness Instructors. ACE Reebok University Press Boston Massachusetts - Publishers .

Elsenvir. Edited b Professor Susan Standing. Gray's Anatomy - September 2008 edition.

Web Sites

Respiratory System
Wikipedia The free encyclopedia
www.en.wikipedia.org

Respiration
The Franklin Institute
www.learn.fi.edu/learn/heart/systems/respiration.html

Anatomy of the Diaphragm
www.A.D.A.M.education.com

Goju Ryu
www.iogkf.com
www.sakura-kai.hu/old/masters.php.

About the Author

Pervez B, Mistry

Shihan Pervez Mistry opened his doors to students of martial arts in 1964, at the age of 19, when he was not much more than a student himself. Judo was his first foray into the mysterious fighting arts of the east; Ju-jitsu, Aikido and ultimately Okinawan Goju-Ryu Karate would follow in a lifetime of teaching and continuous learning. He holds a 4th.degree black-belt in Judo, and a Hachi-Dan (8th degree) black belt in Karate, which was bestowed upon him by his teacher of 35 years, Seiko Shihan (Supreme Master IOGKF) Morio Higaonna, at the tender age of 67 in 2012, in Okinawa, Japan. He is also a Certified Personal Trainer and an Post Rehabilitative Sports Injury Specialist (AFPA) (USA) .

In a teaching career spanning 50 years, tens of thousands students have passed through his doors, many becoming respected teachers in their own right. He has trained the Military and Para Military forces of our country. The Indo-Tibetan-Border-Police, The Border Security Force, The Central Reserve Police Force, The Naval Commandos, The Dogra Battalion of the India Army, The Black Cat Commandos to name a few, making them the battle-hardened fighting forces that they are today.

Now, he is committed to empowering women to look after themselves in a country where women are not respected as they should be. He has travelled the length and breadth of the country conducting seminars on self-defense for women from all walks of life, from the student to the housewife.

Goju Ryu is what he lives and breathes today, unfailingly turning up at the *dojo* thrice a week to impart wisdom and experience culled from a lifetime of blood, sweat and Zen. The Sanchin Kata, which forms the basis of Goju-Ryu training, has always been a subject very dear to his heart. Combining all the resources of tremendous first-hand experience, a keen knowledge of human anatomy, and a wealth of information gleaned over a lifetime in the dojo, he has brought *Sanchin* to the very doorstep of every Karateka who wishes to improve his body, mind and spirit, the three tenets that *Sanchin* is based on.

It is arguable that a better author on the subject could be found, and this book will go a long way in unlocking the inner potential of every student who ever wore a *gi*, irrespective of age and seniority.

He and his wife Zeenat live in Mumbai (Bombay) India.